DEVELOPING AN EFFECTIVE
School Plan

An Activity-Based Guide to Understanding Your School and Improving Student Outcomes

Facilitation Notes

Lori Van Houten
Jeanne Miyasaka
Kim Agullard

with Joy Zimmerman

WestEd, a nonprofit research, development, and service agency, works with education and other communities to promote excellence, achieve equity, and improve learning for children, youth, and adults. While WestEd serves the states of Arizona, California, Nevada, and Utah as one of the nation's Regional Educational Laboratories, our agency's work extends throughout the United States and abroad. It has 14 offices nationwide, from Washington and Boston to Arizona, Southern California, and its headquarters in San Francisco. For more information about WestEd, visit our website: WestEd.org; call 415.565.3000 or, toll-free, (877) 4-WestEd; or write: WestEd / 730 Harrison Street / San Francisco, CA 94107-1242.

ISBN-13: 978-0-914409-36-6
ISBN-10: 0-914409-36-0

Library of Congress Control Number: 2006922973

This book was printed on acid-free recycled paper.

ii

Table of Contents

INTRODUCTION TO FACILITATION NOTES

This volume of *Developing an Effective School Plan: An Activity-Based Guide to Understanding Your School and Improving Student Outcomes* contains the facilitation notes for each activity in the five modules introduced in the *Change Manager's Handbook*. For each activity, these notes review purpose and objectives; provide important background information; list materials you will need, including any overheads, handouts, templates, and resources; identify the approximate time needed for the activity; and give specific directions for the activity. As needed, you'll see directions for what needs to be done in advance, under the heading, "Before the Activity."

Although the facilitation notes refer to overheads, handouts, templates, tools, and other resources (e.g., required readings), such materials are not included in this volume. Instead, you will find them on the CD, which is attached to the inside of the back cover. The CD also includes an electronic copy of the facilitation notes and materials related to the roadmap development activity (Activity 1) presented in the *Change Manager's Handbook*. Directions for using the CD are printed on the last page of this volume, as well as in the Read Me file on the CD itself. The licensing agreement is printed on the inside back cover above the CD.

Prior to reading through each activity identified on your roadmap, you may find it helpful to print any related overheads, handouts, or templates; in this way, you can easily peruse them as they are mentioned in the directions. To make this process a little easier, we have listed, below, each activity and its overheads, handouts, templates, and resources. Also listed are related tools.

Module 1: Get Ready for Inquiry

Activity 1.1: How Data Can Help Us in the School Improvement Process
Overhead 1.1-1: Data-Driven Decision-Making in the Schoolwide Improvement Process
Handout 1.1-1: The Regional Alliance's Top 10 Ways to Use Data as a Lever for Change

Activity 1.2: Unearthing Myths: Challenges to Change
Overhead 1.2-1: Unearthing Myths: Challenge to Change — Purpose
Overhead 1.2-2: Unearthing Myths: Challenge to Change — Guiding Questions
Handout 1.2-1: Excerpt from Setting Our Sights: Measuring Equity in School Change

Activity 1.3: Data for Decision-Making: Emotions, Visions, Opinions, and Understandings
Template 1.3-1 (Examples of Posted Charts)

Activity 1.4: A Matrix for Making Decisions in Our School/District
Template 1.4-1: Matrix of Types of Decisions by Decision-Makers

Activity 1.5: Solve the Puzzle: A System of Data-Driven Decision-Making
Overhead 1.5-1: Purposes of the Puzzle Activity
Overhead 1.5-2: Questions for Teams to Consider as They Design Their System
Handout 1.5-1: Framework for Data-Driven Decision-Making
Handout 1.5-2: Solving the Puzzle: Pieces of a Data-Driven Decision-Making System

Activity 1.6: Creating a Culture of Data-Driven Decision-Making: Reflections on Our Current Inquiry System
Overhead 1.6-1: Reflections on Current Inquiry System — Purposes
Overhead 1.6-2: Reflections on Current Inquiry System — Discussion Questions
Template 1.6-1: Creating a Culture of Data-Driven Decision-Making — Current Inquiry System Practices

X

1

Module 1:
Get Ready for Inquiry

HOW DATA CAN HELP US IN THE SCHOOL IMPROVEMENT PROCESS

Purpose and Objectives

As schools make decisions about action strategies to include in their school improvement plans, several essential broad questions point the way to using appropriate data to make these decisions. Participants will be able to understand

* basic questions involving data that frame the school improvement process, and

* how data can be used as a lever for school change and how these may relate to their own school improvement situation.

Background for Facilitators

Rationale

This activity sets up a framework of the "stages" of data collection and use in making decisions about school improvement. So often, school staff have negative attitudes toward data, especially if the data are not bringing "good news." This activity helps participants understand and think about data constructively.

Source

This activity was developed by WestEd facilitators. It was based, in part, on the work of Nancy Love:

Love, N. (2002). *Using data/getting results: A practical guide for school improvement in mathematics and science* (pp. 28–31). Norwood, MA: Christopher Gordon Publishers, Inc.

Uses

This introductory concept-building activity, intended for the leadership or data team or the full staff, provides a broad overview and links data-driven decision-making work to the school improvement process.

Activity Directions

Materials

⇨ Overhead 1.1-1: Data-Driven Decision-Making in the Schoolwide Improvement Process

⇨ Handout 1.1-1: The Regional Alliance's Top 10 Ways to Use Data as a Lever for Change (3 pages)

Time Required

Approximately 30 minutes

Directions for Facilitators

✱ (5 minutes) Present Overhead 1.1-1 (Data-Driven Decision-Making in the Schoolwide Improvement Process). Describe the role of each question in light of the school improvement process. Point out that data will be needed in addressing the questions.

✱ (5 minutes) Distribute Handout 1.1-1 (The Regional Alliance's Top 10 Ways to Use Data as a Lever for Change). Use the Think-Pair-Share strategy to discuss this article by first asking participants to read it and think about situations in their school that may relate to any of the points ("levers") made in the article.

✱ (5 minutes) In pairs, have participants share and discuss their ideas about "Are any of these levers likely to be barriers to change or ideas for positive change in our school?"

✱ (5-10 minutes) In a large group, have participants share their ideas. Use your group process skills to guide the sharing and discussion in a positive and constructive direction. Given time constraints, this may involve needing to postpone discussion of each idea until all ideas have been shared.

4

UNEARTHING MYTHS: CHALLENGES TO CHANGE

Purpose and Objectives

Using a powerful article on equity and access, participants begin to

* develop a school culture that values data as a tool to support inquiry as a vehicle to ensure educational equity and improve student outcomes, and

* deepen their knowledge of how data can be used to challenge myths and misconceptions that often serve to maintain inequitable or status quo practices.

Background for Facilitators

Rationale

In her book, *Setting Our Sights: Measuring Equity in School Change*, Ruth Johnson stresses the value of using data analysis to "kill myths and build dissatisfaction" and suggests it for motivating staff to identify and support school reform initiatives.

Source

This activity was developed by WestEd facilitators. Excerpted with permission is a passage from: Johnson, R. S. (1996). *Setting our sights: Measuring equity in school change* (pp. 58–61). Los Angeles: The Achievement Council. A new edition of the book is available from Corwin Press: Johnson, R. S. (2002). *Using data to close the achievement gap: How to measure equity in our schools.* Thousand Oaks, CA: Corwin Press, Inc.

Uses

This activity is used with a leadership team or full staff to heighten understanding of how data analysis can uncover myths and misconceptions that often serve as arguments to continue the "status quo" of how business is conducted within our schools.

Activity Directions

Materials

⇨ Overhead 1.2-1: Unearthing Myths: Challenge to Change — Purpose

⇨ Overhead 1.2-2: Unearthing Myths: Challenge to Change — Guiding Questions (3 pages)

⇨ Handout 1.2-1: Excerpt from *Setting Our Sights: Measuring Equity in School Change* (4 pages)

Time Required

35-50 minutes, depending on whether one or more question sets are used

Directions for Facilitators

This activity can be completed in one of two ways: 1) Participants at each table group may read the excerpt from Johnson's chapter and use one set of guiding questions to discuss information and data presented, or 2) a variation of a "jigsaw" approach may be taken, with individuals divided into groups to read the same excerpt but discuss different question sets (three are provided) before returning to home groups to discuss their analysis of the excerpt from the perspective of the different question sets.

* **Before the Activity:** Decide whether one or multiple sets of questions will be discussed. If multiple question sets will be used, create different small groups for reading and discussing and create "home groups" to jigsaw the discussions from each question set.

* (5 minutes) Use Overhead 1.2-1 (Unearthing Myths: Challenge to Change — Purpose) to describe the activity. Tell participants that decisions are frequently driven by myths and assumptions about what groups of students know and are able to do. Explain that using a belief system not grounded in data can take a school reform effort off track. The activity will help the participants look objectively at their beliefs about data and how they are used.

* (20 minutes) Pass out Handout 1.2-1 (Excerpt from *Setting Our Sights: Measuring Equity in School Change*) and display one set of discussion questions from Overhead 1.2-2 (Unearthing Myths: Challenge to Change — Guiding Questions) on the overhead. If more than one set of questions is being used, make handouts instead. Tell participants that they should read the selection with the discussion questions in mind. After 5 minutes, ask participants to share their thoughts with the table group based on the discussion questions.

* (15 minutes for jigsaw only) If different question sets were used, ask participants to return to their home group and share their questions and the gist of the discussion.

* (10 minutes) **Closure:** Debrief the activity with a few groups sharing one aspect of their discussion. Ask, if not already offered, what decisions the participants can think of that have either been based on assumptions or on data, and how they have impacted a reform effort. Make a list of data sources the school could use to avoid relying on myths and assumptions to make decisions. Close by assuring participants that the inquiry the school will engage in will focus on the use of data.

DATA FOR DECISION-MAKING: EMOTIONS, VISIONS, OPINIONS, AND UNDERSTANDINGS

Purpose and Objectives

In this icebreaker activity, participants will

* begin a dialogue to identify concerns, emotions, and knowledge related to use of data for decision-making.

Background for Facilitators

Rationale

Individuals engaging in data-driven decision-making practices bring a variety of emotions, purposes, opinions, and knowledge to their work with colleagues. Identifying people's feelings and their initial knowledge base is essential for leadership teams looking to create a collaborative culture focused on data-driven decision-making.

Being aware of individual concerns, emotions, and knowledge related to data use is an important first step in planning follow-up activities that acknowledge fears and misconceptions about the value of data-driven decision-making, and that build a collective knowledge base about how data-driven decisions can support program improvements.

Source

This activity was developed by WestEd facilitators.

Uses

This activity is often used as an initial icebreaker with full staff or the leadership and/or data team coming together for a first engagement focused on data-driven decision-making. Understanding and acknowledging people's feelings, concerns, and knowledge is an important first step in building a positive collaborative culture and "buy-in" to new practices. Information surfaced during this activity often provides essential information to facilitators for designing next steps to enroll faculty and staff in a positive learning culture focused on ongoing school improvement.

Activity Directions

Materials

⇨ Template 1.3-1 (Examples of Posted Charts)

⇨ Poster paper posted on walls around the room, sticky-note pads on each table, pens, markers

Time Required

Approximately 30 minutes

Directions for Facilitators

✳ **Before the Activity:** Based on Template 1.3-1 (Examples of Posted Charts), prepare four charts to post around the room with questions and statements.

✳ (5 minutes) Ask workshop participants to reflect on the questions and statements posted on the four charts hanging on walls in the room (examples follow).

✳ (10 minutes) Invite participants to respond to at least two of the charts by writing their thoughts on sticky notes (or directly on poster paper with markers if group size is small) and posting on the charts.

✳ (5 minutes) Using a "gallery walk," provide time for participants to read comments from others.

✳ (10 minutes) Ask participants to return to their seats. Review some of the recorded comments and facilitate a brief whole-group discussion soliciting general comments from the group at large.

During the debrief, share the importance of surfacing feelings, knowledge, and concerns about data use to engage all staff in building a collective understanding of the value that data-driven decision-making plays in school improvement. Make sure the following points are made:

— Data to inform decision-making come from a variety of sources such as state, district, and local achievement data; perception data (e.g., surveys); attendance and demographic data.

— It is to our advantage to understand data well so that we know how to effectively use even the data we have concerns about. This is often the case with norm-referenced test data.

— Being attentive to how we collect, summarize, analyze, and interpret data will help us make sound data-driven decisions that support all students' success.

✳ (5 minutes) **Closure:** Remind participants where they are in the inquiry process (e.g., launching a new initiative, revising their plan, seasoned data users) and how important it will be to be objective and use data well in the process.

A MATRIX FOR MAKING DECISIONS IN OUR SCHOOL/DISTRICT

Purpose and Objectives

This activity examines the way decisions are made in a school or a district. In the course of this activity, participants will

* become familiar with the type of decisions made at the site or district, and

* know who participates in making these decisions and at what level.

Background for Facilitators

Rationale

Districts with multiple school sites that initiate site-based decision-making often engage in this activity to clearly define what decisions are made at the district or school level, and which stakeholders have input, a vote, or solely make the decision. Clarity about who makes what decisions is essential so all individuals are clear about their level of ownership and involvement.

Some decisions are clearly mandated by the state in terms of which individual or committee must make the decision. Many other decisions are a balance of ownership, effectiveness, and efficiency. Some types of decisions are appropriate at the district level to be implemented by all schools; other types are appropriate at the school level or teacher level. Those planning the inquiry process should be familiar with this information so they can be sure to have the appropriate data and decision-makers available at each step. The activity may confirm individuals' understandings about the process or identify areas of disagreement or ambiguity. Completion of the matrix may result in a trial process to be revisited after a year or so of implementation.

Source

This activity was developed by WestEd facilitators.

Uses

This activity, used with the full staff, clarifies school and district stakeholders' roles in the decision-making process.

Activity Directions

Materials

⇨ Template 1.4-1: Matrix of Types of Decisions by Decision-Makers

Time Required

Approximately 45 minutes

Directions for Facilitators

✱ **Before the Activity:** Complete several rows of the matrix on Template 1.4-1 (Matrix of Types of Decisions by Decision-Makers) by entering "I" (input) below any role type (e.g., State, Teacher) that provides input (including formal recommendation) for a particular type of decision and entering "D" (decision) below those who *make* the related decisions. If you are sufficiently familiar with the school or district, you can also add in other types of decisions in advance of the activity. Make an overhead and handouts of the semi-completed matrix.

✱ (10 minutes) Distribute the handouts. Explain the purpose of completing the matrix is to familiarize participants with the decisions that are being made and to consider who provides the input and who makes the decisions.

State that this is not meant to be an exhaustive matrix of all types of decisions that will be made in a data-driven decision-making process, but just a sample. An exhaustive process could take from several hours to several days to complete. Using the overhead, ask participants to review the decisions listed on the matrix. Ask for other types of decisions based on the use of data that should be added to the list. Have participants add the new types to their matrix.

Instruct teams to complete the matrix for each type of decision by entering "I" (input) for those providing input, including formal recommendations, or "D" (decision) for those making or approving the decisions. Model this for the first decision on the overhead. Give a time limit of 20 minutes and instruct teams to identify a facilitator and a timekeeper and to reach agreement on all types of decisions within the allotted time.

✱ (20 minutes) Roam among teams to ensure they progress through all types of decisions, entering a question mark where they are unable to reach agreement in a brief amount of time. As they work, ask teams to reflect on changes that may need to be made or structures that must be in place if input is to be received and decisions made (e.g., a parent survey will need to go out before the semester break, data on AP class enrollment must be gathered, the data team will need to meet before the first school board meeting to prepare their recommendation).

✱ (15 minutes) Facilitate whole-group discussion about questions, concerns, and comments. Elicit specific examples of times a decision was made that worked well or failed based on who made the decision and the stakeholder level of involvement.

✱ (3 minutes) **Closure:** State that those responsible for planning the data-driven decision-making process must be aware of where decisions are made and how. By completing the matrix, participants can see the trade-offs in time and buy-in based on who makes decisions. These elements will need to be factored in throughout the inquiry and decision-making process.

SOLVE THE PUZZLE: A SYSTEM OF DATA-DRIVEN DECISION-MAKING

Purpose and Objectives

By creating a system of data-driven decision-making, the facilitator and teams explore what is already known and what needs to be learned before the data-driven decision-making process gets underway. School teams will

* understand the necessary steps and common processes in data-driven decision-making, and

* analyze their own school's process and what strengths and gaps exist.

Background for Facilitators

Rationale

Activating prior knowledge, discovering topics of high interest for learning, and acknowledging participants' strengths are important steps before embarking on complex steps and issues in data-driven decision-making. School communities should understand the full process of data-driven decision-making so they see how the activities they will engage in are all part of a continuous school improvement process and won't see them as discreet activities.

This activity answers the question, "What do you know already?" It is similar to a KWL chart in which small teams fit puzzle pieces together to create a sequential system of data-driven decision-making. The products reflect team knowledge. Misconceptions or knowledge gaps can be addressed during this activity or can inform the facilitator in planning for participants' learning needs.

Source

This activity was developed by WestEd facilitators.

Uses

The activity can be used with the leadership or data team or with the full school staff.

> Note: Products might be saved for later activities. As teams learn new ideas about a system of data-driven decision-making, they might revisit their original products and make revisions.

Activity Directions

Materials

⇨ Overhead 1.5-1: Purposes of the Puzzle Activity

⇨ Overhead 1.5-2: Questions for Teams to Consider as They Design Their System

⇨ Handout 1.5-1: Framework for Data-Driven Decision-Making

⇨ Handout 1.5-2: Solving the Puzzle: Pieces of a Data-Driven Decision-Making System (2 pages)

⇨ Large blank poster paper, glue or adhesive dots for puzzle pieces, markers, pens, scissors, tape

Time Required

Approximately 1.5 hours

Directions for Facilitators

✱ **Before the Activity:** For parts of this activity, the staff will be arranged in small groups. Decide how to organize the groups. Consider having a cross-representation of grade levels and/or subject areas or departments in each group. We suggest trying to keep the groups between 4 and 6 members to facilitate member interaction.

✱ (15 minutes) Begin by distributing Handout 1.5-1 (Framework for Data-Driven Decision-Making).

Explain that our task today will be to create a model of our own data-driven decision-making process. Show Overhead 1.5-1 (Purposes of the Puzzle Activity) and explain that we will achieve our purposes in the course of creating our own model. Using the handout, describe some of the common elements of data-driven decision-making. Highlight the fact that there is no ending point; it is a cyclical process. Remark that this is an example and not all systems have the same components; nor are they all organized in the same way. State that teams may want to revise their charts after exploring steps contained in other workshop modules.

Distribute Handout 1.5-2 (Solving the Puzzle: Pieces of a Data-Driven Decision-Making System), poster paper, and supplies to teams or groups. Designate wall area for the posters. Ask them to cut the puzzle pieces, and explain that they will use them to create a model of the school's decision-making process.

State that teams are free to creatively construct their models. Ask participants to think about decisions made at the school in past years. Who made the decision? What data were used? Was the process linear or cyclic? Tell teams to use the puzzle pieces to create a representation of this decision-making process. Not all pieces have to be used nor does it have to look like the example.

Put up Overhead 1.5-2 (Questions for Teams to Consider as They Design Their System). Give teams a 30-minute time limit to complete their systems posters. Instruct them to answer the two questions as they create their systems and write brief answers on the poster paper. Tell them to write team members' names in the corner of the poster when finished.

✱ (30 minutes) Give teams time to construct their models. While teams work on their puzzle, roam among them. Ask them clarifying questions about placement of pieces but do not advise on construction. The purpose is for teams to construct models based on their own prior knowledge, not for the facilitator to teach.

✱ (15 minutes) After teams are finished, conduct a gallery walk during which they review others' posters. One member of each team might be designated to remain by the team's model to answer visitors' questions.

✱ (30 minutes) Facilitate a group discussion about similarities and differences in the different posters and the two discussion questions. Make a list of elements that everyone wants to be sure are present as they move into a new cycle of decision-making.

✱ (5 minutes) **Closure:** Describe the inquiry or data-driven decision-making process in which the school is about to engage. Talk about how each required element the participants just generated will play out in the process.

CREATING A CULTURE OF DATA-DRIVEN DECISION-MAKING: REFLECTIONS ON OUR CURRENT INQUIRY SYSTEM

Purpose and Objectives

Members from school or district teams reflect on current inquiry system practices, common understandings, and local data-driven decision-making issues, to frame baseline information prior to further planning. At the conclusion of the activity, participants will identify

✴ components of the current inquiry system,

✴ strengths that exist within current practices,

✴ existing challenges or gaps, and

✴ questions, actions, and/or resources needed for further development of the local inquiry model.

Background for Facilitators

Rationale

Identifying components of a local inquiry system and developing a baseline understanding of practice strengths and/or gaps (challenges) is an important preliminary step before embarking on the complex process of data-driven decision-making. It is important that future action steps and engagement in data-driven decision-making activities be informed by a profile of current practices. Additionally, this activity provides baseline information that can be used by teams as a benchmark for future formative assessment while improving (developing) inquiry practices.

Source

This activity was developed by WestEd facilitators.

Uses

This activity is used with the leadership or data team or with the full staff.

Activity Directions

Materials

⇨ Overhead 1.6-1: Reflections on Current Inquiry System — Purposes

⇨ Overhead 1.6-2: Reflections on Current Inquiry System — Discussion Questions

⇨ Template 1.6-1: Creating a Culture of Data-Driven Decision-Making — Current Inquiry System Practices

⇨ Poster paper, markers, pens, tape/tabs for adhering poster paper to the wall

Time Required

Approximately 1 hour

Directions for Facilitators

* **Before the Activity:** Divide the group into teams of 6-8 people and assign different components of a data-driven inquiry system to each team. Components may be personalized to fit the school. Sample components include

  — establishing a culture of data-driven accountability,

  — collection of valid and reliable data,

  — understanding demographic data,

  — understanding achievement data,

  — understanding perceptual data,

  — determining goals and objectives,

  — selecting scientifically based strategies,

  — writing a responsive action plan, and

  — implementing and evaluating an action plan.

  Write the component for each team in the appropriate place on Template 1.6-1 (Creating a Culture of Data-Driven Decision-Making — Current Inquiry System Practices). Make a copy for each team.

  If the school already has a schematic of its inquiry system (generated in Activity 1.5, for example) make an overhead of the schematic or display it in some way (e.g., put the poster up on the wall in the meeting room).

* (10 minutes) Have participants sit in the prearranged teams. Explain that each team will examine a component of the current data-driven decision-making system. If a schematic exists of the school's current system, display this to show the different components. Using Overhead 1.6-1 (Reflections on Current Inquiry System — Purposes), state the importance of developing a common understanding of current strengths and challenges of a data-driven inquiry system prior to engaging in a new cycle of planning.

  Distribute to each team its copy of Creating a Culture of Data-Driven Decision-Making — Current Inquiry System Practices (derived from Template 1.6-1). Point out where the component is that each team will discuss. Using Overhead 1.6-2 (Reflections on Current Inquiry System — Discussion Questions), review the instructions (also listed on the handout) with the teams. Instruct teams to use the discussion questions for their component and record their findings on large chart paper using the handout chart as a model.

  Give time limits (20 minutes to discuss their components) and instruct teams to identify a facilitator, recorder, and timekeeper. Teams should also identify a presenter who will remain with their team's posted information to explain findings to others.

* (20 minutes) Roam around the room to ensure understanding of activity directions and progress in completing the assigned task.

* (15 minutes) Following team brainstorming, conduct a gallery walk in which participants circulate, viewing other charts and asking questions of each designated team presenter.

* (15 minutes) **Closure:** Facilitate a whole-group discussion soliciting general comments. Take the components in order and possibly make notes of changes that will need to be made before engaging further in the inquiry process. In closing, note that periodic formative reviews of changing inquiry practices will be useful in supporting school improvement initiatives.

14

LEADING AND SHARING LEADERSHIP

Purpose and Objectives

High-quality leadership is critical to the success of data-based inquiry and reform efforts. Before embarking on this process, it is important to take stock of the leadership at the school site. As a result of completing this activity, schools will

* affirm the role of strong leadership in increasing student achievement, and

* assess the current capacity for shared leadership at their site.

Background for Facilitators

Rationale

High-quality student performance depends on high-quality school leadership. The critical contribution of school leaders to strengthening student performance was first highlighted through the benchmark research on effective schools in the early 1980s. Then, leadership was envisioned as the role of the principal.

Twenty years later, research and best practices confirm that highly skilled leaders remain crucial to successful teaching and learning. In fact, the principal's impact on student achievement is second only to the influence of teacher quality (Fullan, 2001; Waters, Marzano, & McNulty, 2003; Leithwood, Louis, Anderson, & Wahlstrom, 2004). These studies recognize the critical role of principals in raising student achievement and also move away from the exclusive notion that a school principal can single-handedly provide the instructional leadership to propel an entire school toward educational excellence.

Successful districts and schools know that "leadership is the guidance and direction of instructional improvement" (Elmore, 2000, p. 13). How do high-quality leaders achieve improved teaching and learning? Leithwood et al. (p. 1) suggest that leaders influence student learning "by setting directions — charting a clear course that everyone understands, establishing expectations, and using data to track progress and performance." Therefore, effective leadership extends beyond the superintendent in the district and the principal in the school. Simply stated, "school leadership that must be managed by the principal constitutes only a fraction of the leadership available" (Barth, 2001, p. 446). Effective leadership is distributed among members of the school community and includes assistant principals, teacher leaders, union leaders, board and community leaders, and, in some instances, students themselves. In redefining leadership as broad-based and inclusive, districts redefine who leaders are and who leads (Lambert, 2003). They also redefine the work of instructional improvement and how the work gets done.

Shared or distributed leadership is not merely dividing up the same old workload, but rather it involves taking on specific work together that is focused on improving student learning. Collaboratively, individuals work in teams to plan and execute a series of activities that no single member could accomplish alone (Spillane, Halverson, & Diamond, 2001; Schlechty, 2002). Here, members are not interested in simply getting along. They see their role as contributing their strengths to understanding what needs to be done and on finding solutions in which they can engage all members of the community. The primary team goal is on leveraging all available assets in order to create positive change for students.

15

How do successful districts/schools practice leadership? They adopt a distributed leadership model that uses the expertise and leadership of a number of members, institute a variety of individual leadership roles, and create collaborative leadership structures such as peer learning groups and school leadership teams. They recruit, select, and support leaders who have knowledge about instructional improvement, skills to facilitate groups toward achieving a goal, and a strong conviction that collaboration and teamwork are effective means to increase student achievement.

Sources

This activity was developed by WestEd facilitators.

The Shared Leadership Capacity Survey was developed by Karen Kearney of the Leadership Initiative @ WestEd based on a survey created by the partnership among the School Leadership Team research team at the University of California, Santa Barbara, Gervitz Graduate School of Education, and the state and regional directors of the California School Leadership Academy. This partnership worked with hundreds of school leadership teams in California over 10 years. This assessment is adapted from the partnership's more complex rubric for determining the effectiveness of school leadership teams already formed and working together on school improvement and student achievement goals.

References

Barth, R. (2001, February). Teacher leader. *Phi Delta Kappan, 82*(6), 443–449.

Cleveland Initiative for Education. (2004). *Effective school leadership: Adopting a systemic approach.* Cleveland, OH: Author.

Elmore, R. F. (2000). *Leadership of large-scale improvement in American education.* Washington, DC: Albert Shanker Institute.

Fullan, M. (2001). *Leading in a culture of change.* San Francisco: Jossey-Bass.

Lambert, L. (2003). *Leadership capacity for last school improvement.* Reston, VA: Association for Supervision and Curriculum Development.

Leithwood, K., Louis, K. S., Anderson, S., & Wahlstrom, K. (2004). *Executive summary — How leadership influences student learning.* Minneapolis: University of Minnesota, Center for Applied Research and Educational Improvement; Toronto: University of Toronto, Ontario Institute for Studies in Education.

McKeever, B. and the California School Leadership Academy. (2003). *Nine lessons of successful school leadership teams: Distilling a decade of innovation.* San Francisco: WestEd.

Schlechty, P. C. (2002). *Working on the work: An action plan for teachers, principals, and superintendents.* San Francisco: Jossey-Bass.

Spillane, J. P., Halverson, R., & Diamond, J. B. (2001, April). Investigating school leadership practice: A distributed perspective. *Educational Researcher*, *30*(3): 23–28.

Uses

This activity is used with the leadership or data team. It can be completed before a team is established and periodically thereafter to gauge progress. For a more rigorous assessment, individuals and/or teams can provide documentation that supports each survey response.

Activity Directions

Materials

⇨ Handout 1.7-1: Shared Leadership Capacity Survey

⇨ Handout 1.7-2: Leadership Capacity Survey Analysis

⇨ Poster paper, pencils or pens

Time Required

Approximately 1+ hours — extension activities add 15 minutes each

Directions for Facilitators

✱ **Before the Activity:** Make a poster of Handout 1.7-2 (Leadership Capacity Survey Analysis).

✱ (5 minutes) Review the importance of leadership to student achievement, using the information from the Rationale section.

✱ (5 minutes) Ask participants to think about leadership and how it is currently shared at their site. Tell them they are going to be completing the survey on leadership practices on Handout 1.7-1 (Shared Leadership Capacity Survey). Explain that there are 10 components to rate and that each has 3 descriptions of practice. Ask them to select a description for each of the components that most closely matches the current status of leadership at their site.

Tell participants that they should approach the survey responses from their own individual perspective. Tell them their rating is for leadership as a whole, not just the singular effort of the principal or "best" member of a leadership team.

✱ (10 minutes) Have individuals complete the survey by circling or otherwise marking the box with the most appropriate description.

✱ (5 minutes) When participants have completed the survey, explain that the factors addressed in its questions have been identified in numerous studies as being key to school improvement. Note that the factors fall into two broad categories, one related to the breadth of leadership participation (i.e., principal role, collaborations, group relationships, learning environment that supports diversity, district communications) and the other related to technical skills required for successful execution of leadership decisions (i.e., aligned goals, using data, shared vision, curriculum design and setting standards, and working from research and data). Note that both broad participation in leadership decisions and skillful execution of decisions are representative of strong leadership capacity. For more information on this, refer individuals to Linda Lambert's book in the reference section.

✱ (5 minutes) Pass out Handout 1.7-2 (Leadership Capacity Survey Analysis), and have individuals plot their ratings by indicating each question number in either the High, Medium, or Low box.

✱ (5 minutes) Ask each individual to do a quick analysis of the results:

— Where are most of the ratings for "Participation"?

— Where are most of the ratings for "Skill"?

— Does it seem that their shared leadership capacity is stronger in the Participation or Skill area?

Tell them they can use the notes column on the worksheet to document their response to these questions.

✳ (5 minutes) Have individuals turn to a partner and share results.

✳ (30 minutes) Group Calibration: Ask the whole group to share individual findings, discussing similarities and differences among their ratings. Remind them to use their notes and/or documentation to support their findings. Note results on the poster of Handout 1.7-2 (Leadership Capacity Survey Analysis).

Direct the group to identify three next steps they will take to improve leadership capacity at their site.

✳ **Closure:** Remind the group how important their role is in leading the change efforts at the school. Thank them for their commitment and willingness to take on a leadership role. Note that they will revisit the three next steps over the course of the year.

Extension Activities

✳ (15 minutes) Documentation Notes: As individuals are completing the survey, ask them to note examples of situations or artifacts that support the given rating. Explain that this documentation can be used in discussions with team members later.

✳ (15 minutes) Brainstorm: In addition to the three analysis questions, have participants also consider:

— What are some reasons for low ratings?

— How might these low areas be addressed?

— Who else should be involved in this discussion?

Make notes to share with colleagues at a later time.

ESTABLISHING A SCHOOL LEADERSHIP TEAM

Purpose and Objectives

As a result of completing this activity, schools will

∗ understand the roles and responsibilities of a leadership team and other decision-making bodies at the school in implementing and monitoring a school action plan, and

∗ form a school leadership team (or reconfigure an existing team).

Background for Facilitators

Rationale

This activity helps the school review the makeup and roles of its current leadership team and make adjustments if appropriate. The importance of having a team with the skills and knowledge to lead data-based inquiry and to develop, implement, and monitor a school plan should not be underestimated. The collective force of a well-organized leadership team can bring about sustainable change that benefits all members of the school community (Johnson, 1996; Schlechty, 2002; Spillane, 2001).

Most schools have multiple existing groups that serve a variety of often overlapping functions. For example, there may be a school site council, a literacy task force, a data team, and a principal's advisory council. As an additional outcome of this activity, the participants will ensure that the functions of all these groups are aligned and that their efforts are focused on the development and implementation of a single school plan.

Source

This activity was developed by WestEd facilitators.

References

Johnson, R. S. (1996). *Setting our sights: Measuring equity in school change*. Los Angeles: The Achievement Council.

Schlechty, P. C. (2002). *Working on the work: An action plan for teachers, principals, and superintendents*. San Francisco: Jossey-Bass.

Spillane, J. P., Halverson, R., & Diamond, J. B. (2001, April). Investigating school leadership practice: A distributed perspective. *Educational Researcher, 30*(3), 23–28.

van Heusden Hale, S. (2000). *Comprehensive school reform: Research-based strategies to achieve high standards*. San Francisco: WestEd.

Uses

It is helpful to do this activity with a leadership or data team at the start of a change process or on an annual basis as a way to review and, if necessary, to ensure coordination between leadership groups.

Activity Directions

Materials

⇨ Overhead 1.8-1: The School Leadership Team

⇨ Handout 1.8-1: Defining Current Roles: Leadership Team Task Inventory

⇨ Overhead 1.8-2: Defining Current Roles: Leadership Team Task Inventory

⇨ Handout 1.8-2: Leadership Team Members

⇨ Overhead 1.8-3: Leadership Team Members

Time Required

Approximately 1.25 hours

Directions for Facilitators

✱ (5 minutes) Explain to participants that the goal of the activity is to define the role of their school's leadership team and to recommend leadership team members who can carry out the assigned tasks. Using Overhead 1.8-1 (The School Leadership Team), briefly review the role of the team. Explain that there may be many different teams, individuals, and committees already performing leadership functions at the school and that these groups often have overlapping functions. Having many groups doing the same or overlapping tasks without coordination can undermine the successful implementation of a school plan.

✱ (10 minutes) Give participants Handout 1.8-1 (Defining Current Roles: Leadership Team Task Inventory). Referring to the overhead of the same chart (1.8-2), ask team members to work in pairs or small groups to fill out the second column on the handout to identify which, if any, of the functions are covered by an existing group or individual. Have them leave the last two columns blank at this point. Note that some of the tasks may be shared by several individuals or groups. These should be recorded on the handout.

✱ (10 minutes) Have participants share with the whole group the groups and individuals they have identified on their recording sheets. As the team members report out, have a recorder create a summary version on the overhead or on a computer with an LCD projector.

✱ (5 minutes) Again in partners or small groups, have participants consider whether each task should remain with the existing group or individual, or whether it should be a function of the leadership team, documenting their decision by checking one of the last two columns on Handout 1.8-1 (Defining Current Roles: Leadership Team Task Inventory). Inform participants that they can break tasks up or keep them together. Assure the group that these are not final decisions but a draft set of roles and responsibilities that will be piloted and revised as needed. Have different groups begin with different tasks to ensure that in the allotted 5 minutes someone has considered each task.

✱ (20 minutes) Using Overhead 1.8-2 (Defining Current Roles: Leadership Team Task Inventory) for recording, ask each team to share its conclusion for each task and the basis for making its recommendation(s). Remind the group that this is a draft set of roles and responsibilities that can be revised after a trial period. Move through each task, discussing until there is agreement on which tasks will be the primary responsibility of the leadership team. List any additional tasks the group can think of that the leadership team might need to attend to. At the end of 20 minutes, the group should have a list of tasks its new leadership team will take on.

* (15 minutes) Remind participants that a leadership team needs to represent all constituents of a school community but still be small enough to be effective as a decision-making body — consisting of no more than approximately 12 members. Give participants Handout 1.8-2 (Leadership Team Members). Have participants, working in pairs or small groups, write in the *role* of individuals who would meet some of the criteria for leadership team members. Rather than naming specific individuals, participants should try to use a role (e.g., 2nd grade teacher, parent liaison, principal, social science department head, multilingual resource teacher) since individuals may change while their role will remain. For each one, have them check the relevant descriptor(s) listed across the top of the form.

* (10 minutes) Using Overhead 1.8-3 (Leadership Team Members), go randomly around the room asking each pair or small group to make a recommendation. Put all the recommendations on the form and then discuss whether all these roles are necessary for an effective leadership team. For example, if the focus of the school plan is literacy, it might be more important to keep the literacy resource teacher on the leadership team than a parent liaison or parent representative. Depending on the culture of the school, it might be appropriate to have a larger team in order to build greater leadership capacity, improve communication, and create more "voice" for the school community in the inquiry and change process.

* (5 minutes) Finally, as a group, fill out the bottom of Handout 1.8-2 (Leadership Team Members), indicating when the team will meet.

* **Closure:** Review once again the importance of the leadership team. Remind participants that these are draft agreements that will be revised if needed once the leadership team is functioning. Because some roles are filled by only one person, choosing a role to be represented on the leadership team will effectively identify a particular individual. In cases where several people have the same role (e.g., 2nd grade teacher), volunteers will be sought to represent this role on the leadership team. If no one volunteers or if, conversely, more than one person volunteers, the team will meet again to resolve the issue.

21

DEVELOPING LEADERSHIP FOR COLLECTING AND ANALYZING DATA

Purpose and Objectives

Most schools have a leadership team responsible for organizing, directing, and monitoring school change initiatives. Frequently a subset of this team or perhaps an entirely different group of people will take responsibility for collecting, organizing, and analyzing the data that feed data-driven inquiry. In this activity, participants will be able to

* understand the relationship between the school leadership team and the data team,

* understand the roles and responsibilities of a data team and/or data coordinator, and

* use the suggestions for selecting members of a data team (or, possibly, reconfiguring an existing team).

Background for Facilitators

Rationale

Three elements form the basis of data-driven inquiry — the belief that data are an important and fundamental part of the decision-making process, the commitment to use data in this process, and knowledge of effective strategies for collecting, displaying, and analyzing the data needed. While the leadership team may believe that data are important, and might commit to use data, the team members may not have the necessary skills or knowledge to collect and analyze data. In some cases, it might be wise to have a separate data team or data coordinator to ensure that all three elements are in evidence. In this activity a leadership team, planning team, or even a full staff examines the benefits of having a data team so that data-based inquiry may be more organized, systematic, effective, and enjoyable.

Source

Developed by WestEd facilitators, in part based on the work of Ruth Johnson: Johnson, R. S. (1996). *Setting our sights: Measuring equity in school change*. Los Angeles: The Achievement Council.

A newer version of the book is available: Johnson, R. S. (2002). *Using data to close the achievement gap: How to manage equity in our schools*. Thousand Oaks, CA: Corwin Press.

Uses

The concepts and strategies in this activity are designed for use with the leadership or data team, or the full staff.

23

Activity Directions

Materials

- ⇨ Overhead 1.9-1: Building Capacity: School Leadership and Data Teams
- ⇨ Overhead 1.9-2: The Data Team...
- ⇨ Overhead 1.9-3: Data Team Members

Note: These overheads may also be helpful as handouts.

Time Required

Approximately 30 minutes

Directions for Facilitators

✳ (3 minutes) As an introduction, provide the reasons for building data capability. For ideas, refer to the purpose of this activity and the rationale.

✳ (5 minutes) Present the roles of and relationship between the school leadership and data teams, using Overhead 1.9-1 (Building Capacity: School Leadership and Data Teams). Basically, the school leadership team includes members of the data team. Explain that the school leadership team addresses the broader school improvement efforts and identifies the data needed for planning and decision-making. The data team gathers, preps, and provides the data needed. In some cases, the data team also analyzes the data. Ask if the staff in the school already have assigned data responsibilities. Who does what?

✳ (12 minutes) Present Overhead 1.9-2 (The Data Team...) on the responsibilities and functions of the data team. The following list has language for elaborating on each responsibility or function:

  — *Has formalized, clear responsibility for the data process.* Unless people clearly have the responsibility for collecting, organizing, and displaying data, inquiry efforts may lose focus and be less of a priority.

  — *Is representative of the school community so that different voices or types of expertise are involved in the process.* This is an important way to use people's strengths, experience, interests, and perspectives.

  — *Reports data to the school leadership team and the broader community.* The work and results of the team should be taken seriously because they provide important information for making decisions.

  — *Is organized and meets regularly.* The team should have designated leaders and/or coordinators and various roles for members. The team should have regular meetings so that its work is done in a systematic way.

  — *Is financially supported by funds for planning time, time to collect and prepare the data, professional development, and needed computer hardware and software.* Many schools that have been successful in obtaining and using data have reported that they provide time and compensation for staff who do data work as an integral part of their job, not as something over and beyond their position. Tell participants what resources are available for this.

— *Has a designated coordinator who has assigned responsibilities that are a part of his or her job.* Either inform participants or decide if the coordinator will be paid for this or be relieved of some of his or her duties in order to effectively serve in this position.

— *Builds capacity through professional development.* Professional development is critical to building the capacity of the school or district. Key people need to attend workshops, training sessions, read the literature, etc., to increase their knowledge and skill in data management, analysis, and use.

— *Evaluates the need for outside assistance.* It is important at the outset to determine what kinds of assistance beyond the data team may be needed, and how to locate such assistance. Outside collaborators such as the district or county offices of education, colleges and universities, businesses, evaluators, etc., can be very valuable in providing services needed and possibly building the team's capabilities at the same time.

— *Assesses technological capabilities and needs.* A major obstacle to getting the data is the lack of a comprehensive database necessary for doing important analyses such as disaggregation or determining the characteristics of a particular subset of students. Such data analyses can be effectively accelerated by appropriate technology. School and district leaders need to have serious conversations about the data resources and assistance needed at the school level such as downloading the school's data from the district database into a user-friendly data analysis system. Some schools or districts choose to subscribe to Internet data management and analysis services. Managing the data through and making decisions about a data management system are the purview of the data team.

✱ (10 minutes) Present Overhead 1.9-3 (Data Team Members), which proposes some criteria for selecting data team members. Explain more specifically, that a team may include teachers interested in technology and data use, an administrator, a counselor, a school psychologist, parents, and community members who have data expertise and interest in the school. School psychologists often have knowledge about testing and test scores that can be helpful. The school secretary or a budget staff member may be a helpful member. If the data team is also going to analyze the data, it will be important to have broad representation across grade levels, programs, and subject areas. Have participants begin to think about who might be appropriate members for their school data team.

✱ **Closure:** If the leadership or data team is doing the activity, discuss and determine who will serve on the data team or reconfigured team, respectively. If the full staff is doing the activity, tell them that their nominations for the data team will be considered by the leadership team and the members of the data team will be made known.

TYPES OF DATA AND COLLECTION METHODS

Purpose and Objectives

The purpose of this activity is to help participants understand what data can be used to make school improvement decisions and plans. Participants will be able to

* understand basic types of data, reasons for collecting these data, and examples of each type, and

* understand sources and methods for collecting different types of data.

Background for Facilitators

Rationale

This is an introductory concept-building activity that provides a broad overview and serves as a foundation for school-based inquiry. This activity helps school personnel broaden their concept of data and identify specific types of data that they collect in their school and district. Following this activity, staff will be able to complete the Data Inventory in Activity 1.12.

The concepts learned in this activity will also be important for understanding subsequent activities and processes in this guide, namely the Student Achievement Profiles in Module 2, the investigations of factors impacting student achievement in Module 3, and finally, in monitoring the effectiveness of the school plan in Module 5.

Source

This activity was developed by WestEd facilitators.

Uses

This critical concept-building activity can be used for training the leadership and/or data team. It can also be used with the full staff, especially if the entire staff will be engaged in the data collection and analysis process.

Activity Directions

Materials

⇨ Overhead 1.10-1: Data Quote

⇨ Handout 1.10-1: Types of Data (4 pages)

⇨ Handout 1.10-2: Types of Data (Recording Sheets) (4 pages)

⇨ Handout 1.10-3: Data Collection Methods

⇨ Handout 1.10-4: Data Activity (2 pages)

⇨ Chart paper, markers

Time Required

1+ hours

Directions for Facilitators

✱ **Before the Activity:**

— Decide how to introduce the types of data (see below, Strategies 1 and 2). If choosing Strategy 2, make a separate poster from each page of Handout 1.10-2 (Types of Data [Recording Sheets])

— Read Handout 1.10-4 (Data Activity) to decide whether one of the two school scenarios (elementary or secondary) will be useful with your participants or whether, instead, you would prefer to develop a scenario more appropriate for your context. If you create your own scenario, use those from Handout 1.10-4 as a model.

— Consider inviting the district staff who are in charge of data so they become familiar with the data work and data concepts you are developing with the school staff.

✱ (5 minutes, entire group) Orient participants to the role of data by discussing Overhead 1.10-1 (Data Quote). Point out that data collection can be very time consuming and the amount of available data can be overwhelming. Working smart with data involves good planning to target the essential data needed to make important planning decisions. Consider asking participants about their data work and how it relates to the quote.

✱ (30 minutes, entire and small groups) Pass out Handout 1.10-1 (Types of Data). Tell participants that they will use this information about data in an activity.

— (10 minutes) Orient participants to each type of data by pointing out the "Why collect ....data?" and "What are some examples of ... data?" sections for each type.

— (20 minutes) Help participants better understand and apply the types of data to the school situation by using one of the two strategies suggested below.

Strategy 1 — Small Group Work

Break the whole group into four small groups and instruct them to spend about 10 minutes answering the questions below:

• *How will this data help us to improve our student achievement?*

• *What sources/methods can we use to get this data?*

Ask participants to record their ideas on Handout 1.10-2 (Types of Data [Recording Sheets]), and, for each type of data, ask them to choose a different person to report out to the whole group. As these presenters share their group's ideas with the whole group, record the ideas on chart paper.

Strategy 2 — "Gallery Walk"

Place the four posters of the types-of-data recording sheets that you have prepared in advance on the walls of the meeting room. Place them so there is enough space to accommodate a group of people clustered around each one. Have individuals or small groups walk around the room to look at the posters. Have them take and refer to their copies of Handout 1.10-1 (Types of Data) and Handout 1.10-3 (Data Collection

Methods) as they consider and write their responses to the two questions on each poster. Encourage and facilitate discussion among participants. Allow approximately 10 minutes for this part of the activity.

The following suggestions are for helping participants process their ideas after the gallery walk: Have them look for common themes; ask them which of the items on the list they have done or would like to do; ask them what sources/methods for getting data they already have or would like to have. Have participants share out their observations. Participants can record ideas on Handout 1.10-2 (Types of Data [Recording Sheets]).

✱ (30 minutes, entire and small groups) Apply the types of data by doing a data activity from Handout 1.10-4 (Data Activity) to help participants apply the types and specific kinds of data to school scenarios. Choose the scenario most relevant to participants or use one you have developed in advance to better reflect participants' context.

Give each group a copy of the scenario. Instruct the groups to use Handout 1.10-3 (Data Collection Methods) as a source of ideas for questions to investigate and to determine data needed for their scenario. Have groups work on the scenario for about 15-20 minutes and monitor or facilitate the groups.

With the entire group, ask each small group to report out, responding to the following questions: *What questions did you suggest to investigate? What data did you select for investigation and why?* Record some of their responses on the overhead or on chart paper.

✱ (5 minutes) **Closure:** Use Overhead 1.10-1 (Data Quote) again. Tell participants they are just getting started with data-based inquiry and that, ideally, as a result of this activity they have a better idea of what data can and should be used to answer their inquiry questions. Tell participants that they will be working more closely with data to investigate their students' achievement and the factors that affect student achievement and, then, once the plan is written, to monitor effectiveness of implementation.

29

VALIDITY AND THE DATA-DRIVEN DECISION-MAKING PROCESS

Purpose and Objectives

Using data to make decisions is for naught if the data are not valid for their intended purpose or if they are not appropriate or adequate for making a particular decision. As a result of this activity, participants will be able to understand

* the concept of validity, and

* the role and function of validity in the data-driven decision-making process.

Background for Facilitators

Rationale

This activity develops a basic knowledge base about the credibility and use of data. A good understanding of validity is very important in ensuring that data users know how to evaluate and select appropriate data to investigate questions about student achievement and why it is the way it is. The findings from investigations are used to justify decisions on strategies, practices, or programs the school may want to initiate. When data are inappropriately used, people often blame the data rather than the use of the data. This frequently results in a resistance that can "close the door" to using data to make decisions. Moreover, people sometimes blame the data if they don't *like* the decision, even if the data were appropriately used. Understanding the role of validity in selecting and using data for inquiry purposes can help avoid these setbacks to developing an effective school plan.

Source

This activity was developed by WestEd facilitators with contributions from Karen Poppen of the Beaumont Unified School District, Beaumont, California.

Uses

This critical concept-building activity can be used for training the leadership and/or data team. It can also be used with the full staff, especially if the entire staff will be engaged in the data collection and analysis process.

Activity Directions

Materials

⇨ Overhead 1.11-1: Data/Decision Scenario

⇨ Overhead 1.11-2: Data

⇨ Overhead 1.11-3: Validity

31

⇨ Overhead 1.11-4: Validity and the Data-Driven Decision-Making Process

⇨ Handout 1.11-1: Validity and the Data-Driven Decision-Making Process

⇨ Handout 1.11-2: Validity Considerations for Using Data (2 pages)

⇨ Poster paper, broad felt-tip markers (1–2 for each table), tag board or construction paper, scissors

Time Required

Approximately 1 hour, depending on participants' examples and questions

Directions for Facilitators

✱ **Before the Activity:**

— Divide the group into small groups of approximately 4 people.

— This activity has several parts. For the opening activity, make sentence strips (approximately 20 inches by 3 inches) from tag board or construction paper. Make enough strips so that each group of 4 participants will have 5 strips and there will be some extra strips for those groups that want more. Right before the meeting, put 5 strips and 1–2 markers on each table.

— For the third part of this activity, "Introducing the Concept of Validity," make 3 posters, one for each aspect of validity in Overhead 1.11-4 (Validity and the Data-Driven Decision-Making Process). In the upper one-third of each poster, write the validity aspect (e.g., validity of the data and results from assessment instruments) and the question related to that aspect. Leave the rest of the space for participants to tape their sentence strip responses from the opening activity.

✱ (15-20 minutes, entire group and small group) **Opening Activity.** Begin by telling participants that in using data to make decisions, they need to be sure to use the right data to make the right decisions. Connect this activity to prior data work or situations in the school to build local context and importance.

Using Overhead 1.11-1 (Data/Decision Scenario), explain that participants are looking at a piece of data from an elementary school and the decision that was made based on the data. Tell participants that in their small group, they should discuss the following questions:

1) *What are some concerns you might have about this decision?*

2) *What questions do you have about this situation?*

Identify someone in each group to share out the group's concerns and questions.

Instruct participants to work in their small group (of about 4 people) for 5 minutes to discuss concerns and questions related to the scenario. Instruct them to write each concern or question on a strip of paper. Tell them that they will use these strips later.

With the entire group, ask small group presenters to share out their concerns and questions.

✱ (10 minutes, entire group) **Introducing Concepts About Data.** Tell participants that, as they can see from the opening activity, simply taking a piece of data and using it to make a decision can be problematic.

Start the discussion by refreshing or augmenting people's understanding of what data are (and are not) by showing Overhead 1.11-2 (Data). Elaborate on the quote by explaining that data are facts or figures to be processed: evidence, records, statistics from which conclusions can be inferred. Data can be both numerical (quantitative) or word-based (qualitative). Data have no meaning in and of themselves. They are neither good nor bad. They have meaning only when we interpret and use the data in our particular context.

Put Overhead 1.11-1 (Data/Decision Scenario) up again and review the data:

> Data: *20% of the 5th graders scored in the lowest proficiency level on the state reading test in 2006.*

Then explain how two different groups might interpret the data differently:

> Interpretation of staff in School A: *"We did very well! The rate in the lowest level dropped from last year — let's celebrate."*

> Interpretation of staff in School B: *"We didn't do well. Twenty percent in the lowest level is not good for our students. We need to do better."*

✳ (20 minutes, entire group) **Introducing the Concept of Validity.** Using Overhead 1.11-3 (Validity), point out that when we use data to make decisions, we want to be sure that the data themselves are "valid," that is, credible or trustworthy. We also want to be sure that the data we use are "valid" for the decisions being made.

Pass out Handout 1.11-1 (Validity and the Data-Driven Decision-Making Process) and Overhead 1.11-4 (of the same name) to discuss the points about the three aspects of validity in the data-driven decision-making process. For each, ask the small groups to contribute their concerns or questions (from the paper strips) that are relevant to the aspect. Carefully monitor the examples they give to be sure they accurately represent the point being made.

— **Aspect 1. Validity of data and results of assessments:** Do the *results* or data from assessments (e.g., tests, survey questions, observations) really represent what the assessments are *supposed* to measure? [*Notice that it is the results and data that are valid, not the instrument itself.*]

Point out that the state reading test is generally supposed to be a broad measure of the reading content standards indicated in the test blueprint. Test items are generally reviewed for alignment to the standards and blueprint to ensure that the test results are valid.

Have the participants review their concerns and questions from the opening activity and ask if any of them relate to this validity question. Tape relevant examples (on the sentence strips) on the poster. Some examples may be:

— *How many items on the test assessed decoding?*

— *How did our students score on the decoding items?*

— *How did students do in other reading areas?*

— **Aspect 2. Validity of interpretations and conclusions drawn from the data:** Tell participants that this aspect of validity focuses on the accuracy of the interpretations and conclusions based on the data. Are the interpretations and conclusions accurate and supported by the data?

Point out that, sometimes, the data may be valid but people make inferences or draw conclusions that are not accurate; that is, they are not supported by the data.

Have the participants review their concerns and questions from the opening activity and ask if any of them relate to this validity question. Tape relevant examples on the poster. Some examples may be:

— *How was it decided that decoding was the area of need?*

— *Maybe that 20% was largely English learners who need an emphasis on vocabulary building, not decoding.*

— *How are the other 80% of the students doing? What are their strengths and weaknesses?*

— **Aspect 3. Validity in use of data to make decisions:** Are the decisions based on adequate and appropriate supportive evidence? Emphasize that when we use test scores and other data to make decisions, we need to be sure we are using the appropriate data and enough or sufficient data to make the decision. Stress that we need to examine the data carefully to be sure they accurately and fully represent our decision targets.

Have the participants review their concerns and questions from the opening activity and ask if any of them relate to this validity question. Tape relevant examples on the poster. Some examples may be:

— *Why decoding as the emphasis? Do they need decoding?*

— *Was the decision based on the results from one test?*

— *What other reading assessment information do they have?*

— *What are the demographics of the students in this group?*

— *Why are only these students in intervention?*

— *It is too much of a "blanket fix."*

✱ (15-20 minutes, entire group and small groups) **Apply the Validity Concept in Data Use Situations.** With the entire group, review the top portion (questions A, B, and C) on page 1 of Handout 1.11-2 (Validity Considerations for Using Data). Then, instruct participants to work in their small group and match the six examples provided with the appropriate validity consideration question. Allow about 2-3 minutes for participants to do the match in their small group; then, with the entire group, have the participants share their answers. You may want to use the answer key on page 2 of the handout as an overhead for this portion of the activity.

✱ (5 minutes) **Closure:** If appropriate, ask participants to think about and share situations from their school that relate to the validity considerations and questions above. For example, teachers have a critical role in making sure that the student demographic and program information are accurate (Situation A). Remind them that when they take this role seriously and provide or check the information carefully, they are contributing to the validity of the information in test results. Remind them that this will be very important as the school moves through the inquiry process to identify needs, choose appropriate solutions, and implement and monitor their school plan.

CONDUCTING A SCHOOL DATA INVENTORY — WHAT DATA DO WE HAVE AND NEED?

Purpose and Objectives

Knowing what data you have, where they are, and what shape they are in is a major first step in the data collection process. The purpose of this activity is to introduce strategies and tools for conducting an inventory to determine what data in the school and district are readily available, somewhat available, and not available. Participants will be able to

* understand why schools should conduct a school data inventory, and

* apply strategies for focusing a data inventory.

Background for Facilitators

Rationale

Many schools do not know what data they have, the data format, or who has the data. The data inventory is an important step in knowing what data are available and ready for analysis and use in decision-making and school improvement planning.

The School Data Inventory tool provided in this activity includes data that are helpful for making some of the basic decisions to optimize school functioning and planning. The data are listed by the types discussed in Activity 2.1. At first glance, the amount of data in the inventory may seem overwhelming. *It is not necessary or recommended for a school to complete this profile all at once!* However, remember that this is an inventory, and strategies to identify data priorities will be provided in this activity.

Source

This activity was developed by WestEd facilitators.

Uses

This activity can be used with the leadership or data teams.

Activity Directions

Materials

⇨ Overhead 1.12-1: Knowing What Data You Have

⇨ Handout 1.12-1: Getting Started with Data

⇨ Overhead 1.12-2: School Data Inventory — Purpose

⇨ Handout 1.12-2: School Data Inventory — Purpose

35

⇨ Handout 1.12-3: School Data Inventory (10 pages)

⇨ Handout 1.12-4: A Strategy for Focusing Your Data Inventory

⇨ Handout 1.12-5: Analyzing the Results of Your Data Inventory

⇨ Your School Improvement Plan (If using this activity with school teams)

⇨ Chart paper, markers, tape

Time Required

Two sessions: approximately 1.25 hours for Session 1, and 35-45 minutes for Session 2. The time can vary greatly depending on how much time facilitators or school teams take to discuss the questions, identify needed data, focus their inventory, and/or actually start their school inventory. The second session should be held after the school data inventory has been completed.

Directions for Facilitators

Session 1 — Introducing the Data Inventory Concept and Starting the Inventory Process (approximately 1.25 hours)

* **Before the Activity:**

  — Identify and invite the participants (i.e., leadership team, data team, key district office staff responsible for school data) to the meeting.

  — Talk with key people in the school about some of their data successes and problems so you will have a good context for facilitating the meeting.

* (2 minutes) **The Rationale for Data Management.** Open the meeting by showing Overhead 1.12-1 (Knowing What Data You Have). Tell participants the purpose of the meeting.

* (15 minutes) Pass out Handout 1.12-1 (Getting Started with Data) and introduce it by telling participants that this first activity will help them get a handle on the status of the data and the use of data in their school. The questions raise good points for discussion to help school teams start their data work. With the entire team (if the team is small) or in small groups, have the participants discuss and answer as many questions as they can. Write the responses on chart paper and post the chart(s) so you can refer to it in the next activity. (Type the responses later to use in future data meetings.)

* (5 minutes) **The Concept of the School Data Inventory.** Use Overhead 1.12-2 (School Data Inventory — Purpose) and corresponding Handout 1.12-2 to introduce the concept of and rationale for a school data inventory — what is it, why do it, and who should do it? Refer to some of the responses in the "Getting Started with Data" portion of this activity as a rationale for taking an inventory of the school data.

* (30-45+ minutes, depending on how much work is done at this meeting) **Conducting a School Data Inventory.**

  — (5 minutes) To the entire team, distribute and introduce Handout 1.12-3 (School Data Inventory) by noting that the sections of the inventory are based on the types of data (i.e., demographic; student achievement; curriculum, instruction, and program; perception) reviewed in a previous activity (Activity 1.10). Orient participants to the inventory directions and form by reviewing the directions on the first page of the handout, then showing how these terms are used as column headers in the inventory form. Point out that each type of data is made up of categories, such as Student Enrollment, Attendance, and Behavior (indicated in bold capital letters). A data category (e.g., Behavior) may involve several more specific kinds of data (e.g., suspensions, expulsions). Tell participants that the specific kinds of data are typical of what schools have and that they can add others that are of particular interest to their school. Give participants a few minutes to look over the inventory.

— (20+ minutes) Develop a rationale for focusing the inventory process by mentioning that, at first glance, the amount of data in the inventory may seem overwhelming. *Stress the idea that it is neither necessary nor recommended for a school to complete this profile in one sitting!* Tell them that the main idea is to determine what data are most needed and most available. Distribute and discuss Handout 1.12-4 (A Strategy for Focusing Your Data Inventory).

Present the first focus, *readily available data*, then have the participants look at the School Data Inventory tool and write a checkmark to the left of the data they know they already have.

Present the second focus, *school improvement plan data related to the goals, objectives, and strategies*. Participants should make sure that these are checked in the school data inventory so that the data will be collected.

Present the third focus, *school program evaluation data needs*. Have the school teams make a list of the federal, state, district, and/or school programs, and explain that they should determine what data they need for reporting and evaluation purposes. They should determine the data they will need about each program and check off these data on the list in Handout 1.12-3 (School Data Inventory). Depending on the amount of time available for the meeting, this part may be done after the meeting.

Finally, schools may have a *problem area* they want to investigate. In the alternative, this portion of the activity may be done by selected participants after the meeting. Have school teams talk about whether they have a problem area in their school that needs investigation and identify potential data they may need.

Note: If school staff members are planning to write a grant proposal, they should think about what data they need to include in the proposal.

— (10-15 minutes) Develop a plan for getting the information about each needed piece of data that was checked. Tell participants that some data may be needed for more than one purpose. These will obviously be high priority data. Have participants decide who will find the data information to fill out the columns in the inventory form. Have people volunteer, or make assignments, so that someone is responsible for making sure that the task gets done. The school team may want to divide the inventory work by type of data. Also make sure that people agree on a completion date for the inventory. Schedule a date for the next meeting to analyze the results of the inventory.

— **Closure:** Summarize the decisions regarding who will collect information and by when. State the next meeting date.

Session 2 — Analyzing the School Data Inventory Results (35-45 minutes)

﹡ **Before the Activity:** The leadership or data team or selected individuals should prepare the results of the data inventory by filling in the form (Handout 1.12-3 [School Data Inventory]) and making copies to hand out.

﹡ (30-40 minutes) **Analyze Results from Data Inventory.** Review the data inventory and discuss the guide questions in Handout 1.12-5 (Analyzing the Results of Your Data Inventory). Write the responses, issues, problems, etc. that arise during the discussion on chart paper and post them on the wall.

Next Steps: Develop strategies and plans to address important data collection issues and problems. Make sure the plans include persons responsible for each task and the completion date.

﹡ (5 minutes) **Closure:** Take the time to acknowledge the work and the people involved in the inventory process. Debrief with participants about the process and their accomplishments.

Module 2:
Organize & Analyze Data

ANALYZING TABLES AND GRAPHS TO CREATE DATA STATEMENTS

Purpose and Objectives

To understand and effectively use student achievement data, educators must be able to analyze and describe test results. In this activity, participants will learn strategies to

* analyze the student achievement data provided in the tables and graphs, and

* write descriptive statements about results.

Background for Facilitators

Rationale

When school staff initially review tables and graphs displaying student achievement data, conversations can immediately turn to explanations for specific data points: "I'm sure we didn't cover that part of the curriculum before the test. No wonder the scores went down." Or, "That class had fewer English learners this year than last. I'm not surprised there were gains." Letting the data tell the story rather than relying on hunches and assumptions leads to a more accurate analysis of student needs and provides a reliable base for constructing a responsive action plan. A series of investigations and analyses would need to be done to validate the hunches shared above. Writing data statements, or factual descriptions of findings observed in the data, is the focus of this activity and the first step in an accurate analysis of root causes for student achievement.

In this activity, specific questions are provided to construct data statements and guide analysis of student achievement data. School teams can use the questions to look at and think through the student achievement information portrayed in the tables and graphs. They learn how to "write up" the results in statements that describe the main ideas and trends, with supportive details that are directly related to the data. Teams also learn how to distinguish between findings directly reported in the data and inferences or explanations based upon data. Because creating data statements is a time-consuming and detailed task, we recommend the leadership and/or data team complete this activity. Full staff time is better used in the next step of looking across data statements to identify patterns and trends.

Finally, this activity is designed to align with the tables and graphs generated by the Excel templates in Tool 2.1a (Developing a Student Achievement Profile). Guiding questions to help write data statements are organized by the template modules, but they are also relevant for any data source or set of tables and graphs. If Tool 2.1a is not being used, facilitators may wish to review and possibly reorganize the questions to fit the data tables and graphs being used in a current investigation.

Source

This activity was designed by WestEd facilitators. The "Guide for Describing Meaningful Differences in Overall Achievement Test Results" you'll find in this activity was developed by John Carr, WestEd, and is described in his book, Carr, J., & Artman, E. (2002). *The bottom-up simple approach to school accountability.* Norwood, MA: Christopher Gordon Publishers.

Uses

This activity is for the leadership and/or data team.

Activity Directions

Materials

⇨ Overhead 2.1-1: Types of Student Achievement Results

⇨ Handout 2.1-1: Analyzing Student Achievement Results: Guide Questions and Sample Statements of Results and Findings (5 pages) (Print this handout on a different color paper.)

⇨ Overhead 2.1-2: Describing Versus Interpreting Data

⇨ Handout 2.1-2: Sample Data Pages with Findings (4 pages)

⇨ Handout 2.1-3: Guidelines for Writing Statements of Results and Findings

⇨ Handout 2.1-4: Guide for Describing Meaningful Differences in Overall Achievement Test Results (2 pages)

⇨ Overhead 2.1-3: Focus Areas (optional)

⇨ Template 2.1-1: Format for Data Page

⇨ State or district student achievement results from criterion-referenced or norm-referenced tests (use graphs and charts created with Tool 2.1a or provide your own)

Time Required

2-3 hours, depending on amount of data and size of team

Directions for Facilitators

* **Before the Activity:**

— To begin this activity, determine which achievement data will be analyzed (e.g., district-level tests, state criterion-referenced test [CRT], norm-referenced test [NRT] achievement results).

— Make copies of the tables and graphs of student achievement test results created using Tool 2.1a (Developing a Student Achievement Profile: Excel Templates) or those generated by the district or school for the basic types of student achievement areas (i.e., students tested; overall achievement; quartile group achievement [NRT] or proficiency group achievement [CRT]; school, district, state achievement comparisons; demographic group achievement [disaggregated achievement]). Insert the pertinent tables and graphs on Template 2.1-1 (Format for Data Page). Leave the findings and summary sections blank.

— If necessary, modify Overhead 2.1-1 (Types of Student Achievement Results) to match the types of data you will be using in the activity.

— For the section of the activity in which participants practice writing data statements, choose one of the sample data pages provided in Handout 2.1-2 (Sample Data Pages with Findings). Make a copy of the relevant sample for each participant.

— If there are a lot of data to analyze, it may be wise to divide the task among the team: For example, you may decide to give math to one group, and language arts to another. It may also make sense to give proficiency data to one group and school, district, and state achievement data to another. After you review the amount of data for analysis and the time available for the activity, decide how to organize the small groups for data distribution. Depending on the size of the leadership or data team, a "small group" might be two team members or a group of four to five.

✱ (10-15 minutes) **Orientation to Data Analysis**. Using Overhead 2.1-1 (Types of Student Achievement Results) — modified, if necessary, to match the data your school will use — review the type of data the teams will be analyzing today.

Inform participants that after you have reviewed the processes, they will be analyzing data and writing descriptive statements.

Using the tables and graphs provided by your district or from Tool 2.1a (Developing a Student Achievement Profile: Excel Template), orient participants to reading the title and legends and other descriptive labels, so they can understand the types of data that are reported, for what groups and/or grade levels, what years, and any other descriptive information.

Refer to Handout 2.1-1 (Analyzing Student Achievement Results: Guide Questions and Sample Statements of Results and Findings) and explain its relationship to the tables and graphs you will use for this activity. Point out that there is a title on each page that indicates the focus of the questions (e.g., A. Students Tested, B. Overall Student Achievement). Note that each page is organized the same way, with single-year questions and sample data statements on the top half and multi-year questions and sample data statements on the bottom.

Identify the data analysis areas and questions that participants will be reviewing. Point out that the data analysis questions are just examples of key things to examine in the data analysis. Depending on the data analysis purpose, a few of the questions may not be appropriate to address at that particular time.

For example, if you are only reviewing reading achievement results, then the questions that ask about comparing the results of other subject areas are not relevant at this time. Instead, focusing on the differences among the grade levels may be more important. Some of the questions ask about meeting your student achievement goals. Use these in your analyses, if you have such goals.

✱ (10 minutes) **Overview to Writing Data Statements.** Tell participants they will be learning how to write a data statement, that is, a descriptive report of the facts or an objective observation of what the data actually say. Stress that this is a literal reading rather than an interpretive one. To illustrate the difference, use Overhead 2.1-2 (Describing Versus Interpreting Data), explaining differences between "describing" results and "interpreting" results. Read the first and second examples aloud and explain them, then use the rest as a teaching tool. Read them one at a time, covering the ones you have not yet come to. Ask a volunteer to explain why a statement is descriptive or interpretive. Discuss to ensure everyone understands the concept and can discriminate between the two.

43

✱ (20-30 minutes) **Model and Practice Writing Data Statements.** Tell participants that you will first model how to create a descriptive statement using the data display they have. Place the data display you will be using for this teaching session on the overhead and talk aloud as you orient yourself to the chart.

For instance, using the high school example in Handout 2.1-2 (Sample Data Pages with Findings), say: *This table is for the CST English/Language Arts test for 9th, 10th, and 11th graders. It shows the percent of proficient students by grade level both at our school and the state for 2003, 2004, and 2005. So, what is this telling me? Let's start with 9th grade. In 2003, 32% of our 9th grade students were proficient on the CST English/Language Arts test. In 2004, the percent proficient decreased to 31%, and in 2005 it increased to 37%. So, a data statement that captures this is:*

"From 2003 to 2005, the percentage of proficient students increased by 5 percentage points on the 9th grade CST English/Language Arts tests: from 32% in 2003 to 31% in 2004, to 37% in 2005."

So let me see if I have all the information I need in this statement. (Refer to Handout 2.1-3 [Guidelines for Writing Statements of Results and Findings].) *Are facts stated objectively? Is the statement short and clear in everyday language? Is it understandable standing alone? Are there relevant numerical data? I think it meets all of those criteria.*

I think I will make another statement comparing the school and state pattern across years:

"From 2003 to 2005, on the 9th grade CST English/Language Arts test the percentage of proficient students at our school increased 5 percentage points (32% to 37%), which is the same increase as for 9th grade students across the state (38% to 43%)."

Let me see if I have all of the information I need in this statement. (Use Handout 2.1-3 again.) *Are facts stated objectively? Is the statement short and clear in everyday language? Is it understandable standing alone? Are there relevant numerical data? I think it meets all of those criteria.*

Ask if there are any questions about how the statements were formulated.

Next, ask someone to volunteer to form a data statement about the school data. Record the statement on chart paper, prompting with questions to ensure that all parts are included. When done, have participants use the guidelines to check the statement.

Ask if there are any questions. Repeat at least one more time until participants are comfortable with writing data statements.

Pass out Handout 2.1-4 (Guide for Describing Meaningful Differences in Overall Achievement Test Results). Tell participants that, when analyzing achievement across several years to determine progress, people often want to know if the gain or loss is "statistically significant." Determining statistically significant differences would need to be done by a data-savvy person who is knowledgeable about the various statistical tests and their requirements. However, this handout can help participants determine in a much more general way how meaningful the changes in their test scores may be, based on how many students were tested. Tell them that the procedure can only be used with percentage scores, such as the percentage of students who met or did not meet a proficiency standard or the percentage of students who scored at/above or below the 50th national percentile. Using the high school example in Handout 2.1-2 (Sample Data Pages with Findings), walk participants through the decision of whether or not the change in performance for the 9th graders is a meaningful difference. (With more than 500 students in the two years and a 5 percentage point difference, this is a "small" difference.) Ask participants to calculate the difference for the change in the 10th and 11th grade percent proficient.

Next, have the participants work in pairs to write a statement about an agreed-upon portion of the school data. Have them write their data statement on a piece of scratch paper. Next, have them check it against the guidelines.

Ask a pair to volunteer to read their statement. Record it on a piece of chart paper. Lead the participants through the guidelines to evaluate the statement. Correct if necessary. Ask another pair to volunteer. Record and repeat the process until participants feel confident.

Tell participants that it isn't important to write every possible statement about a data set, but to write those statements that capture key elements of the data. Refer to the sample statements to illustrate the point.

✱ (30 minutes-1 hour, small groups) **Analyze Student Achievement Results.** In the groups determined before the activity, have participants analyze data in the tables and graphs by using Handout 2.1-1 (Analyzing Student Achievement Results). Using the completed data pages prepared before the activity using Template 2.1-1 (Format for Data Page), have the groups write statements of findings in the space provided. If more space is needed, they can continue on the back of the sheet. Circulate among the groups and monitor the creation of the data statements and participants' discussion. For the sake of accuracy, be sure to correct errors in terminology such as "increased by 5%" instead of "increased by 5 percentage points." If they have used the term "significant difference," ask them to explain how this was determined.

> **Note: Analyzing Disaggregated Student Achievement Results**
>
> The data-analysis guiding questions for demographic and program subgroup achievement from page 5 of Handout 2.1-1 (Analyzing Student Achievement Results) can be used with all disaggregated student demographic characteristics such as gender, race/ethnicity, economic status, mobility status, English proficiency, and special education students.

✱ (10-15 minutes, small groups) **Review Findings for Accuracy and Clarity.** After participants finish their data analysis, have them exchange with another group to review their findings for accuracy and clarity. Use Handout 2.1-3 (Guidelines for Writing Statements of Results and Findings) as a checklist for the review. Emphasize that they should make sure that the statements accurately represent the data and are clearly understandable to any reader. Remind participants that there are many statements that could be written about a set of data. Groups should not check that every possible statement has been written, but that the existing statements meet the criteria.

✱ (10-15 minutes) **Closure:** Ask each group to share a data statement from the data they have reviewed. Reiterate how this factual description of the data is a first and crucial step in the analysis process. Explain that the next step will be to bring these statements to the full staff for further analysis. Staff will create summaries using the statements this group has generated.

Note: Focus Areas

Focus areas serve as headers for related sets of findings in the student achievement data and as an organizer for both the ongoing investigation into root causes and the subsequent school plan. The focus areas need to be selected and the data pages organized under each header prior to the next activity (2.2) when participants will create data summaries. In many cases, there are predetermined focus areas. For example, often a state or district process requires particular sections of a school plan to be written around math and language arts. In this case, the facilitator and/or leadership or data team only need to organize the data pages under each focus area. Another possibility is that after the initial review of the data in this activity there will be clear evidence of discreet areas of need. As an extension of this activity, the leadership or data team can identify focus areas and organize the related data pages under them from aggregated to disaggregated. Use optional Overhead 2.1-3 (Focus Areas) if you wish to introduce focus areas here and have the participants organize the data pages under each one. If you choose to select focus areas as part of this activity, note that it is possible to have a data page fit under more than one heading. For example, disaggregated language arts data might fit with a language arts focus area as well as under the English learners focus area.

ANALYZING DATA STATEMENTS TO CREATE FOCUS-AREA SUMMARIES

Purpose and Objectives

To make effective decisions about strategies, programs and practices, educators must have a clear sense of student learning needs. The full staff needs to grapple with the achievement data — identifying the patterns, trends, and relationships across a variety of assessment results to be prepared for this decision-making. In this activity, participants will learn strategies to

✱ identify patterns, trends, and relationships across data statements created in Activity 2.1, and

✱ write descriptive summaries reflecting the key findings in the student achievement data.

Background for Facilitators

Rationale

Before moving further in the inquiry process, the full staff must understand and begin to take responsibility for their student achievement results. Without this level of understanding, staff can make decisions based on beliefs and assumptions and not based on the challenges portrayed in their achievement data. Faculty and staff conversations about student achievement results can be exciting and constructive. However, if the test results are not positive, if a collaborative culture has not been established, or if staff have little experience in talking about data, these conversations can also be difficult. It is important to engage in a process that makes a distinction between ideas that are data based and ideas based on biases and assumptions, as schools summarize and distill the major points in their achievement data.

This activity is a carefully constructed culmination to examining student achievement data. Participants are first introduced to the notion of a focus area and how the data pages have been organized under each heading. The focus areas provide a heading for the primary challenges noted in the achievement data and serve as organizers for subsequent research into root causes and identification of strategies to address those needs. Then, participants complete a data summary for a set of findings from a single data page (see Activity 2.1 for the development of a data page). They are taught to write summaries that are objective and that focus on the key findings. Finally, participants create a focus-area summary that provides a snapshot of both the challenges and the strengths found in the achievement data for that focus area. To make sure the activity goes smoothly and to meet the objectives, read all of the instructions carefully before doing the activity and pay particular attention to the "Before the Activity" instructions.

In this activity the facilitator plays a key role in keeping the staff focused on the data and the task at hand. You must also stop participants from generating solutions for a perceived problem or jumping to conclusions about the "whys" and reasons for the student achievement; identifying the whys occurs later in the process. Facilitators must also keep the focus on improvement rather than on attributing blame. It is also important to keep a balance between "bad news" and "good news." Based on knowledge of

47

the school context, if serious conflicts are expected, the facilitator should consider bringing in a skilled outside facilitator and/or appropriate in-house people.

Finally, this activity represents the culmination of the study of achievement data. There will be some significant findings to share with the school community when this activity is completed. It is recommended that the leadership or data team meet following the activity and decide which stakeholders need information and how it should be shared with them. Tool 2.2 (Communicating with Constituents) provides a format for planning how to communicate the outcome of this activity; it is equally useful for other activities throughout the planning and implementation process.

Source

This activity was developed by WestEd facilitators. The "Guide for Describing Meaningful Differences in Overall Achievement Test Results" was developed by John Carr, WestEd, and is described in Carr, J., & Artman, E. (2002). *The bottom-up simple approach to school accountability.* Norwood, MA: Christopher Gordon Publishers.

Uses

This summarizing process was designed for use by the full school staff. It is designed to facilitate the understanding of relationships and patterns across data statements.

Activity Directions

Materials

⇨ Handout 2.2-1: Focus Areas

⇨ Overhead 2.2-1: Focus Areas

⇨ Overhead 2.2-2: Describing Versus Interpreting Data

⇨ Overhead 2.2-3: Sample Data Pages With Findings and Summary (4 pages)

⇨ Handout 2.2-2: Procedures for Writing a Data Summary

⇨ Handout 2.2-3: Guide for Describing Meaningful Differences in Overall Achievement Test Results (2 pages)

⇨ Handout 2.2-4: Sample Data Pages With Findings and Summary (4 pages)

⇨ Template 2.2-1: Data Summary

⇨ Completed Data Pages with findings from Activity 2.1, copied as handouts and overheads

⇨ Overhead 2.1-2: Types of Student Achievement Results (optional)

⇨ Blank paper, pens, poster paper, markers, highlighters

Time Required

Approximately 2.5 hours

Directions for Facilitators

✳ **Before the Activity:**

— In planning this activity, be sure to include whoever participated in Activity 2.1 because they will be most familiar with the school data. Based on your knowledge of the school context, decide what role these key people will play in the activity.

Note: Focus Areas

Focus areas need to be identified as an organizer for both the ongoing investigation into root causes and the subsequent school plan. As mentioned in the rationale, the focus areas need to be selected prior to the activity, with the data pages from Activity 2.1 organized under each one. In many cases, there are predetermined focus areas. For example, often a state or district process requires particular sections of a school plan be written to address math and language arts. In this case, the facilitator and/or leadership or data team only needs to organize the data pages under each focus area. Another possibility is that the initial review of the data in Activity 2.1 will have provided clear evidence of discreet areas of need. If so, the leadership or data team can identify focus areas at the close of Activity 2.1 and organize the data pages. Finally, the facilitator and/or leadership or data team can identify the focus areas and organize the data pages under each one prior to the activity. Note that it is possible to have a data page fit under more than one heading. For example, disaggregated language arts data might fit with a language arts focus area as well as under the English learners focus area. Also note that at the end of this activity, if desired, participants can take their broad focus area (e.g., math) and give it a more descriptive title (e.g., minority math achievement) to better reflect the summary.

— Make sure the focus areas have been selected and that the data pages from Activity 2.1 have been appropriately organized behind them, from aggregated to disaggregated.

— Decide if all focus areas will be considered in one session or if you will address only one focus area per session. The decision will be based on the time available for the session, the amount of data and number of findings, and the experience of the faculty in dealing with data.

— Make copies of the data pages from Activity 2.1 to be used in the session (one copy per two people). Paperclip them together or put them in a folder so participants can review them side by side if needed. Also, make an overhead of the same data pages.

— Decide whether it would be helpful in Step 1 of Set the Stage to use Overhead 2.1-2 (Types of Student Achievement Results) from Activity 2.1. If so, prepare the overhead.

Note: Unless otherwise noted, the instructions in this activity assume you are dealing with only one focus area per session and, thus, that participants are all using the same set of data pages. It is possible to deal with multiple sets of data in the same session, but the instructions would need to be revised accordingly.

— For parts of this activity, the staff will be arranged in small groups. Within each group, they will work mostly in pairs and occasionally as a small group. Decide how to organize the groups. Consider having a cross-representation of grade levels and/or subject areas or departments in each group. We suggest keeping the groups between 4–6 to facilitate member interaction. If you are addressing more than one focus area, each group will be assigned a different focus area.

— Use Template 2.2-1 (Data Summary) to prepare a data summary form by filling in the title of the focus area to be addressed in this activity. Make an overhead and poster of the form, as well as handouts.

✱ (35 minutes) **Setting the Stage — 4 Steps**

(10 minutes: Step 1) Review the activities and accomplishments of the leadership and/or data team. Describe the types of data the group reviewed, including the specific assessment(s). Use an overhead to show a sample of the original tables and graphs the group used. It may be helpful to use Overhead 2.1-1 (Types of Student Achievement Results) provided in Activity 2.1 to assist in this explanation. Describe the process the group followed to create a data page with the data statements. Explain how the data statements were created. (The goal is to help staff feel comfortable that the data statements are a faithful representation of the data.) Have different members of the leadership and/or data team talk about the process.

(10 minutes: Step 2) Using Handout 2.2-1 (Focus Areas) and corresponding Overhead 2.2-1, explain the definition of a focus area, what the focus areas are for this school, and how they were determined. Describe how the data pages have been placed with the focus area they will be addressing.

(5 minutes: Step 3) Put up the overhead of the blank data summary page for the focus area being discussed. Tell participants they will create summaries for data statements on individual data pages in the focus area. Then, they will look across these summaries to identify patterns and relationships, which they will capture in focus-area summaries.

(10 minutes: Step 4) Stress that the summaries they will create today are literal rather than interpretive. To illustrate the difference, use Overhead 2.2-2 (Describing Versus Interpreting Data), to talk about the differences between "describing" results and "interpreting" results. Read aloud and explain the first two as examples, then use the rest as a teaching tool: Read the examples one at a time, covering up the ones not yet used. Ask a volunteer to explain why a statement is descriptive or interpretive. Discuss to ensure that everyone understands the concept and can discriminate between the two types of statements.

✱ (20-30 minutes; large group) **Practice Writing a Data Summary.** For this portion of the activity, in which you'll demonstrate how to write a summary of data statements, you'll be using page 1 (Achievement Data: State Math Test Proficiency Level Results — 2003–2005) of Overhead 2.2-3 (Sample Data Pages With Findings and Summary). Cover the summary section of the page when you display the overhead.

After passing out Handout 2.2-2 (Procedures for Writing a Data Summary), ask participants to review the findings on the overhead for Achievement Data: State Math Test. Explain that this *review* of findings (i.e., data statements) is the first in a three-step procedure for writing a data summary, as explained in the handout. Make sure they understand how the findings were derived from the data in the table above the findings.

Remind participants that some data may look more important than they are. Distribute Handout 2.2-3 (Guide for Describing Meaningful Differences in Overall Achievement Test Results). Explain that when analyzing achievement across several years to determine progress, people often want to know if the gain or loss is "statistically significant." Determining whether differences are statistically significant would need to be done by someone who is knowledgeable about the various statistical tests and their requirements. Explain, however, that the guide in their handout can help them determine in a more general way whether changes in test scores are meaningful based on how many students were tested. Tell them the guide can only be applied with percentage scores, such as the percentage of students who did or did not meet a proficiency standard or the percentage of students who scored at/above or below the 50th national percentile. Using a different example from Overhead 2.2-3 (Sample Data Pages With Findings and Summary), one that gives the numbers of students and provides data by percentages, demonstrate how to use the guide to gauge how large a difference is. Point out the reference to the guide that is included in Handout 2.2-2 (Procedures for Writing a Data Summary).

Explain that the next step is to organize the findings. Noting that the example on the overhead is of a single subject (math) across years, explain how you know this to be the case. Then, explain that in summarizing, you need to organize data statements or findings from the general to the specific: starting with big, broad ideas about the whole group (e.g., school-level analysis), moving to a deeper, more-specific grade-level analysis, and then moving to an analysis of subgroups within grade levels.

The next step is to write the data summary. To prepare them for this step, have participants talk with the person next to them about summarizing the main points they see in the findings on the overhead. Suggest that they make notes about key points, data, or phrases from the findings that they might want to include in a summary. Have them jot down a draft summary on blank paper.

After all the partners have completed their drafts, uncover the summary on the overhead and discuss it in relation to the Procedures for Writing a Data Summary. Ask for volunteers to share and discuss their own summary. (The aim is for participants to be able to identify the most important data statements and include them in the summary along with pertinent data.)

Using additional examples from Overhead 2.2-3 (Sample Data Pages With Findings and Summary), again walk participants through the steps for writing a summary. Repeat until they are comfortable with the summarizing process.

✱ (30-45 minutes, depending on number of data pages; large group) **Write Data-Page Summaries.** Ask participants to work in pairs, and give each pair copies of the school data pages from Activity 2.1. Tell them they are going to use the process they learned in the prior part of this activity to write data-page summaries. Remind them they can consult Handout 2.2-2 (Procedures for Writing a Data Summary) and Handout 2.2-3 (Guide for Describing Meaningful Differences in Overall Achievement Test Results). Pass out Handout 2.2-4 (Sample Data Pages With Findings and Summary) as well, noting that they might want to refer to some of the summaries to see how they are crafted and how the statements were derived from the data.

Make sure all the pairs have their data pages organized from the aggregated to the disaggregated. Then, have them take the top (most aggregated) page, study the data statements on it, and write a summary. They can write the summary on bottom of the data page or, if there is no room, on a separate sheet of paper.

When all pairs have had time to complete a summary of the first data page, display the overhead of the same data page. Then, ask for a volunteer pair to share its summary. Record the summary on the overhead and have the whole group check it for accuracy and completeness. Ask if anyone would like to add to it. When the whole group agrees that the summary is acceptable, pass out copies of the data summary form (created from Template 2.2-1) and have each participant record the agreed-upon summary under the heading "Individual Data-Page Summaries." The facilitator or an assigned note-taker should also record the summary on the poster-sized versions of the data summary form that were created in preparation for the activity.

> Note: There must be enough identical posters so that each small group has its own poster in the "Write Focus-Area Summaries" part of this activity.

Repeat this process until there is an agreed-upon summary for each of the data pages and participants have documented the summaries on their data summary forms for the focus area in question.

> Note: If you want to have participants address multiple focus areas during this session, assign participants to focus-area groups and appoint a facilitator for each one. Have pairs in each group draft a summary for each data page associated with their focus area and then have each focus-area group reach agreement on a single summary for each data page. Roam around the room making sure each focus-area group is on task and that the summaries adequately reflect the data descriptions. Have the groups document their final summaries on their poster of the data summary form.

✱ (30 minutes; small groups) **Write Focus-Area Summaries.** Break participants into pre-assigned small groups. They will start by working in pairs within those groups. Explain that in this portion of the activity, pairs will look across the data-page summaries and distill their main points from the data-page summaries to create a focus-area summary. Have them refer to the individual data pages, the data summaries the whole group agreed on, and Handout 2.2-3 (Procedures for Writing a Data Summary). Tell them to organize their focus-area summary similarly to how they organized their data-page summary, from the broad (or the aggregated) to the specific (or the disaggregated). Explain that it can be helpful to highlight key points in each summary.

After each pair has created a focus-area summary, have them share within their small group and come to agreement about a final summary to share with the large group. Have each group write its agreed-upon summary on its poster. Note: If you are dealing with multiple focus areas in one session, break participants into their pre-assigned focus-area groups and then follow the directions above.

✱ (20 minutes; large group) Have participants take a 10-minute gallery walk to review and compare focus-area summaries. Encourage participants to document any questions or hunches they have on sticky notes and place them on the data summary poster. Ask them to note any additional "digging deeper" questions, especially about student populations, enrollment, attendance, and program (e.g., English learners, special education), or questions that would require additional disaggregation (e.g., achievement in language arts by language proficiency). The questions or hunches may move beyond description, into interpretation. Tell participants they are capturing these now so they are not lost, but that they will be investigated later in the process as staff look at root causes of their student achievement.

After the gallery walk, work with the full group to reach consensus on one focus-area summary that best captures the main ideas, or combine several summaries to create one final summary. Emphasize the need to be descriptive, not interpretive. Tell participants that the next steps will involve trying to better understand the reasons behind the results.

Note: If several focus areas are being addressed in one session, have participants do a gallery walk following the instructions above. After the gallery walk, ask participants to comment on what they saw in the different focus-area summaries. Expect responses about seeing similar or contrasting findings across focus areas, the need for additional information, comments about the validity of assessments, and suggestions for ways to address challenges. If no one volunteers a comment, read some of the sticky notes on the posters to generate a short discussion. Emphasize the need to be descriptive, not interpretive.

✱ (10 minutes, large group) Ask participants if they would like to add further description to the title for their focus area so it better reflects their focus-area summary. Suggest the title "Minority Math Achievement" as an example. Show how adding more description in the title reflected a shift in the focus area from something broad (math) to something more specific, as called for by the findings themselves. Ask the whole group for suggestions for the title of their focus area.

✱ (5 minutes; large group) **Closure:** Publicly recognize the hard work of the staff and different teams that have collected and analyzed the data to this point. Explain that this represents a turning point in the investigation phase of the planning. The next step will be to investigate the factors that produced the student achievement results they have been discussing. Tell participants that any additional questions they have raised will be addressed as they look at root causes for their student achievement.

54

Module 3:
Investigate Factors Impacting Student Achievement

RESEARCH-BASED FACTORS THAT AFFECT STUDENT ACHIEVEMENT

Purpose and Objectives

School staff should consider factors that research has shown to affect student learning to help them develop an understanding of their current level of student achievement. This activity provides schools with a research-based framework for exploring possible causes for their student achievement and subsequently making school improvement decisions. Participants will

* become familiar with factors that research shows affect student achievement,

* understand that these factors represent common characteristics and practices of effective, high-performing schools, and

* begin to discuss how these factors affect their school's current level of student achievement.

Background for Facilitators

Rationale

This concept-building activity helps schools focus on factors that research has shown to affect student achievement. Before venturing into investigating their school's current level of student achievement, it is wise to build a conceptual framework to serve as a guide. When trying to explain their student achievement level, staff will often turn to factors over which they have little control (e.g., poverty, student mobility). Staff may also focus on factors that research has shown to have little impact on achievement (e.g., attending conferences, new playground equipment, a single session of professional development). Additionally, it is important to demonstrate to staff that student achievement can improve, and further, that there is substantial evidence that certain factors have greater impact than others. This activity will create a positive outlook for the staff as they begin their journey into digging deeper into the factors driving their student achievement.

Source

This activity was developed by WestEd facilitators. Sources for articles used in this activity are listed under *Materials*.

Uses

This introductory concept-building activity is designed for use with the full staff.

57

Activity Directions

Materials

⇨ A selection of the following articles or readings:

— Reading: 3.1-1: American Educational Research Association. (2004, Fall). Closing the gap: High achievement for students of color. *Research Points*, 2(3). Available at http://www.aera.net/publications/?id=314

— Reading: 3.1-2: American Educational Research Association. (2004, Winter). English language learners: Boosting academic achievement. *Research Points*, 2(1). Available at http://www.aera.net/publications/?id=314

— Reading: 3.1-3: American Educational Research Association. (2005, Summer). Teaching teachers: Professional development to improve student achievement. *Research Points*, 3(1). Available at http://www.aera.net/publications/?id=314

— Reading: 3.1-4: Reeves, D. (2000). 90/90/90 Schools: A case study. Chapter 19 in *Accountability in action: A blueprint for learning organizations* (2nd Ed.). Englewood, CO: Advanced Learning Press. Available at http://www.makingstandardswork.com/Downloads/AinA%20Ch19.pdf

— Reading: 3.1-5: Almanzán, H. M. (2005, Summer). Schools Moving Up. *Educational Leadership, 62*. Available at http://www.ascd.org/portal/site/ascd/menuitem.5e54c45350be7c4fb85516f762108a0c/. Click Archived Issues; click Summer 2005, Turn Around Schools.

— Reading: 3.1-6: National Study of School Evaluation. (2004, September). *Technical guide to school and district factors impacting student learning*. Schaumberg, IL: Author. Available at http://www.nsse.org/resources_tools/Tech_Guide.pdf

— Reading: 3.1-7: National Center for Educational Accountability. (2002, July). *The Broad Prize for Urban Education: Showcasing success, rewarding achievement*. Austin, TX: Author. Available at http://www.nc4ea.org/files/9_13Broad.pdf

With the exception of Reading 3.1-7, these articles are available on the CD. Reading: 3.1-7 is available at the related url. Please let participants know that all readings are included with permissions of copyright holders.

⇨ Overhead 3.1-1: Some Factors That Influence Student Achievement

⇨ Handout 3.1-1: Definitions of Factors That Influence Student Achievement

⇨ Sticky notes (2 colors); flipcharts, chart paper and markers; highlighters

Time Required

2+ hours

Directions for Facilitators

The recommended articles relate to the various factors that affect student achievement. By becoming familiar with these key factors, participants begin to think about how their own practices relate to each factor and may affect student achievement at their school.

The following table indicates the factors (A–I) highlighted by each article.

Resource Article	A. Curriculum	B. Instruction	C. Assessment	D. Professional Development/ Collaboration	E. Leadership/Focus	F. Staff Expectations	G. Parent Resources	H. Student Resources	I. Issues of Equity
Closing the Gap: High Achievement for Students of Color (AERA)	X	X			X	X			X
English Language Learners: Boosting Academic Achievement (AERA)		X	X						X
Teaching Teachers: Professional Development to Improve Student Achievement (AERA)		X		X					
90/90/90 Schools: A Case Study (Reeves)	X	X	X	X	X				X
Schools Moving Up (Almanzán)	X	X		X	X	X	X		
The Broad Prize for Urban Education: Showcasing Success, Rewarding Achievement (NCEA)	X		X	X	X				
Technical Guide to School and District Factors Impacting Student Learning (National Study of School Evaluation [NSSE])	X	X	X	X	X	X	X	X	X

✱ **Before the Activity:**

— Select appropriate readings from the suggested list or choose others that are appropriate for your context. Determine how many groups you will need and whether each group will read different articles, more than one article, and/or if more than one group will read the same article. Make sufficient copies of the articles.

— In addition to determining groups for the readings, make tentative groupings for discussing each factor. Try to put people together who have read different articles to provide a richer discussion. The groups may need to be revised depending on the number of findings or questions posted on each factor chart.

— Prepare one chart-paper poster for each factor covered in the article(s) you have selected. Use the factor as the title for the poster.

✱ (5-7 minutes) Explain that this activity is a preliminary step to answering the question: "Why is our school's student achievement at its current level?" Tell them that research on effective high-performing schools has identified characteristics and practices common across these schools. The articles they will be reading discuss these common factors.

Begin by posing the question, "What factors support the achievement of all students?" Participants may do a "Think-Pair-Share" activity or jot down individual "Quick Writes" and share their ideas within their table group. Participants may record their responses in journals or on scratch paper, for future consideration.

✱ (15 minutes) Distribute Handout 3.1-1 (Definitions of Factors That Influence Student Achievement) and display Overhead 3.1-1 (Some Factors That Influence Student Achievement). Ask participants to think about their responses to the previous question and consider which factors their responses address.

Allow a brief amount of time for table talk so that participants become familiar with the factors.

As participants share ideas with their table groups, post the factor charts around the room. Also, make sure that two colors of sticky notes are on each table, along with highlighter markers.

✱ (20-30 minutes) Distribute articles according to the plan created before the activity. Tell participants that as they read an article, they should individually highlight the important research findings and consider what *surprised* them but they understand to be correct, what *affirmed* or reinforced what they already knew or believed, and what they *questioned* (i.e., doubted). They should record each finding on a separate sticky note, using color #1 for findings that surprised them or affirmed their thinking and using color #2 for findings they have questioned. Have them indicate on the sticky note the article from which the finding is drawn.

✱ (10-15 minutes) In reading groups, have individuals take turns sharing one of their sticky notes, telling tablemates if the research surprised them, affirmed what they knew, or if they questioned the finding. Have each table group agree on three to five findings to share with the whole group, including one that they questioned. Have them prepare to present the findings and identify the factor(s) to which they relate.

✱ (20-30 minutes) With the whole group, briefly model selecting a finding on a sticky note and, placing it on a factor poster, explaining why you put it with that factor. Then have each reading group report one finding and post it on the appropriate factor chart. "Popcorn" around the groups (calling on them in random order around the room) and repeat until all main findings are posted. Ask for additional research findings that individuals feel are important, and post them on the charts. Do the same for the finding that each group questioned.

If there are a number of "color #2" question sticky notes questioning a finding, determine if this is an issue or finding about which participants need greater understanding. You may post it in a "parking lot" (i.e., chart paper placed in a corner of the room for later attention), or you may need to deal with it at this time. Find out if it's a common disbelief and why it is questioned. Ask participants if additional information about the issue might have been offered in a different article.

If there are any findings that don't fit with one of the factors being considered, reach an understanding of how to expand a factor so that the finding is represented or create an "other" category and put this in the parking lot to be revisited later.

✱ (20-30 minutes) Re-group participants into the "factor groups" determined before the activity. You may need to reconfigure the groups somewhat, depending on the number of findings or questions on each factor.

Have groups use the factor-specific posters you prepared in advance and brainstorm ideas about how their assigned factor applies to their school, asking themselves, "Based on research findings, where does our school stand in terms of this factor? How do we know? What is the evidence?"

Have groups record their ideas on their factor poster and relate them to specific sticky note findings. Caution them to look beyond assumptions and/or isolated cases (i.e., exceptions, one-time cases). This information provides a preliminary look at additional issues participants may need to consider (e.g., the need for more research on a topic) as a lead-in to Activity 3.2.

✱ (15-20 minutes) Facilitate a whole group conversation, having participants look for underlying themes across factors — consistent threads, commonalities, etc. — so that they can begin determining which factors affect student achievement at their school.

This search for common threads may be prompted by a reflection question (e.g., What underlying themes do you find across factors?) or participants may focus on one factor of their choosing, asking, "What does this factor mean for our school?"

✱ (5 minutes) **Closure:** Explain to participants that they should keep these factors in mind as they move through the inquiry process. These factors will provide them with a framework for focusing further data inquiry and for understanding their student achievement results.

CONNECTING RESEARCH-BASED FACTORS WITH OUR STUDENT ACHIEVEMENT

Purpose and Objectives

As they move forward in the continual school reform process, schools will examine the factors that impact their student achievement to identify needs and guide future decisions. The article(s) in the previous activity provide a picture of the practices related to each factor that effective schools use to leverage change. In this activity, participants will

* formulate hunches about the relationship between their student achievement and factors presented in Activity 3.1, and

* write hunches in the form of questions to investigate in order to determine improvement needs.

Background for Facilitators

Rationale

School staff have ideas about what is impacting student learning and achievement. These hunches, accurate or not, many times guide their behavior. In this activity, using a "fishbone chart" as part of the inquiry procedure, staff surface and share their hunches. In addition, the factors described in the articles in Activity 3.1 are used as a way to broaden staff's thinking about what may be impacting student learning, asking them to consider curriculum, instruction, and assessment, as well as expectations and equity issues. The emphasis is on broadening their understanding of the factors impacting student achievement and focusing attention on factors for deeper investigation over which the school has influence. Because this activity leads to an investigation phase conducted by a subset of the staff, it is important that the full staff understands as an outcome of this activity the direction and purpose of the subsequent investigations.

Source

This activity was developed by WestEd facilitators.

Uses

This activity is designed for use with the full school staff.

Activity Directions

Materials

⇨ Overhead 3.2-1: Some Factors That Influence Student Achievement

⇨ Handout 3.2-1: Definitions of Factors That Influence Student Achievement

⇨ Template 3.2-1: Fishbone Activity for Focus Area

⇨ Overhead 3.2-2: Example of a Completed Fishbone

⇨ Factor posters with findings, questions, and notes from Activity 3.1

⇨ Data Summary pages and posters with focus area and data-page summaries from Activity 2.2

⇨ Chart, overhead projector, markers, sticky notes, pens, staff sets of stickers (dots) in three colors

Time Required

2 to 2.5 hours

Directions for Facilitators

✱ **Before the Activity:**

— Using Template 3.2-1 (Fishbone Activity for Focus Area), make a handout for each focus area you will be addressing. On each one, write the name of one of the focus areas and, below it, transfer the information from the related Focus-Area Summary created in Activity 2.2. In the empty boxes on the fishbone, add any other factors you think appropriate to consider (e.g., others from Overhead 3.2-1 [Some Factors That Influence Student Achievement], different factors that apply to your school). Create an overhead of one of the focus-area fishbones to use as an example or, if you prefer, use a modified version of Overhead 3.2-2 (Example of a Completed Fishbone), which focuses on minority math achievement. If you use this example, modify the overhead by deleting the questions on the fishbone.

Also, for each focus area you will address, create a large fishbone poster that includes the focus area title and the factor you have filled in the box for each bone.

— Assign participants to small groups of 3-5. If there are only one or two focus areas, have all small groups complete the activity for all focus areas, allowing approximately 20 minutes per focus area. If there are more than two, it may be best to start different groups on different focus areas and then have them pass around the fishbone form. For example:

> *For 5 focus areas, divide participants into 5 focus-area groups. Have one fishbone prepared for each of the five focus areas. Assign one focus area to each group. No group will have the same focus area. Give the group 20 minutes to brainstorm hunches in the form of questions and record on their poster. At the end of the 20 minutes, have them pass along the forms so each group has a different focus area than last time. This time give them 15 minutes to add any additional hunches. Rotate again, this time giving 10 minutes. Continue this until all groups have had all focus areas, reducing the time allotted to 5 minutes for the next two rotations.*

— Post around the room the factor posters from Activity 3.1.

Note: The facilitator directions are written assuming that there are at least three focus areas and the same number of working groups. If there are one or two focus areas, the facilitator will need to take participants through the same conversations, but as a whole group. A recorder will take notes on the fishbone poster chart for the focus area. No rotation will be necessary.

✳ (5 minutes) Describe the three steps in the activity for participants: Explain that during this activity they will consider how different factors may be impacting their current student achievement. Use Overhead 3.2-1 (Some Factors That Influence Student Achievement) to provide context. Explain that the first step is to formulate hunches, in the form of questions, about the relationship between their student achievement and the factors. These questions will be used to guide the investigation that will help determine improvement needs. Next, participants will review all of the questions and select the three for each focus area that are most likely to produce the greatest information about why their student achievement is as it is. Finally, they will produce groups of related questions to help streamline the investigation.

✳ (15 minutes) Using the same overhead (3.2-1), ask participants to recall their previous readings and discussions of the factors that impact student achievement. Bring their attention to the factor posters around the room from their work in Activity 3.1. Remind them of their discussions of the factors and the factor definitions by giving them a quick verbal tour of the posters, highlighting the findings, questions, and additional notes about the factors as appropriate. Do a "whip" around the room to gather ideas from participants about the articles from Activity 3.1, the questions they raised during that activity, and the factor definitions in Handout 3.2-1 (Definitions of Factors That Influence Student Achievement). Answer any questions necessary to clarify what is meant by each factor.

✳ (10 minutes) Refer to the data summary posters for each focus area from Activity 2.2. Ask for a volunteer to review how the data summary statements were created. Remind staff of the questions they posted about the data. Highlight a few. Let them know that they will now revisit these questions in greater depth. Explain that staff will generate hunches, in the form of questions, for each focus area around the factors they just reviewed so the school can learn more clearly about why their achievement is the way it is.

✳ (10 minutes) Tell participants they will create some hunches together as a group before working in small groups. Put up the overhead of the fishbone you created or use Overhead 3.2-2 (Example of a Completed Fishbone). Model what they will be doing in the group. Think aloud as you do this. For example, if you are using Overhead 3.2-2, you might say:

Focus area: Minority Math Achievement in High School

Factors: Curriculum, Instruction, Assessment, Issues of Equity, Staff Expectations, Student Resources

OK, first I want to review the focus-area data summary. (Read summary) Now, what are some hunches I have about why these data are the way they are? I wonder how curriculum is impacting our minority students' math achievement? I think our kids don't come to us with the math background they need to take our math classes. I need to restate this hunch as a question. So … I wonder how well the math curriculum in middle school is preparing our students to do high school math? That goes under curriculum. Now I also think that our students are having problems with reading the math textbook. So… I wonder if our students can read at the grade level expected in the math texts? I also wonder if our instructional strategies really engage students, and if they tap into higher-order thinking skills? Sometimes I don't think our students care about math. So, where can I put this? Student resources. What do our students think about themselves as learners? As mathematicians? I wonder if our students feel we think they are capable of being good students? Hmm … I wonder if all staff think our minority students are capable of doing well in higher math classes? (As you state each question, place it on the appropriate fishbone.) I don't think our African American students are enrolled in higher-level math courses at the same rate as the white and Asian students. There is no place to put these enrollment questions so I'll ask about that in the empty fishbone.

Next, ask the staff to share some of their hunches. Guide them in formulating their hunches as questions. Point out the phrasing — "I wonder if," "why," or "how" — as a way to make their hunch into a question. Encourage them to ask questions about curriculum, instruction, students, and teachers since this is what they have the most chance of influencing. The questions need to push the investigation deeper, getting under the surface to reveal the real problems that must be addressed. The aim here is to get information about the root causes that can then be addressed to improve student learning and achievement.

✳ (15 minutes) After there are questions under each heading, ask staff if they are clear on how to generate the hunches as related to factors. Ask someone to describe how to change a hunch into a question. Ask others to add on to this explanation. Ask if there are any questions about how to do this. If not, explain how the activity is organized (see "Before the Activity" guidance on assigning groups and focus areas). Tell them if they have hunches that don't fit into the factors listed on the fishbone, to make additional lines, label them, and add the hunch/question. Advise them that this is not the time to get into a discussion about the hunch. They should not go off on tangents about a particular area, but stick to the activity. Also, tell them not to judge any hunch. All ideas are welcomed.

✳ (20 minutes to 1 hour, depending on the number of groups and focus areas) Tell groups they have 20 minutes for the first focus area. Begin the activity. Circulate around the room, going to each group to make sure they are all doing the activity correctly. Stop and reteach if more than two groups are doing the same thing incorrectly. Call time and rotate posters. Ask if there are any questions. Tell them not to worry if they didn't get to all factors; their colleagues will now build on what they have listed. Continue until all groups have had an opportunity to list questions for each focus area.

✳ (20 minutes) Explain to staff that now that they have had the opportunity to discuss and generate some questions for each factor, the next step is to select the factors and the specific questions for the investigation. Give each staff member three stickers of different colors per focus area. (So, if there are four focus areas, each participant will have 4 red, 4 yellow, and 4 blue stickers.) Tell them now that they have had the opportunity to deeply consider the factors related to the focus areas, they will prioritize the factors for further investigation. This will help to focus their "digging deeper" investigation. Assign a value to each color sticker. For example, red means it is their first priority, yellow second, and blue third. Tell them to walk around the room and on each focus group poster place three stickers next to the factors they think are the most important to investigate. This choice of factors is determined by answers to the following questions: What factor will give us the most insight into what is happening with student achievement improving in this focus area? By working through which of these factors do we have the greatest chance of improving student achievement in the focus area? Direct them to place their dots next to the factors in each focus area as guided by these questions, indicating their first, second, and third priority.

✳ (15 minutes) Briefly review the fishbone posters. Walking around the room, mark or highlight in some way the three factors that will be further investigated in each focus area. Tell participants that for each factor that will be investigated further, they will now combine, cluster, and prioritize the questions to streamline the investigation. Explain that the leadership team will design the investigation into each factor and that this clustering will help them in that task.

Using Overhead 3.2-2 (Example of a Completed Fishbone), review the questions under one factor. Ask if any of these questions are related, if they pose a similar question, or if they pose a question that could be answered using similar data. For example:

> *The questions about instructional strategies for engaging students and the one about tapping into higher order thinking skills are related, so I will highlight these with a yellow pen to show they are related. I also think the questions about students' thoughts about themselves as a learner and about themselves as a mathematician are related so I will highlight them with another color.*

* (20 minutes) Give each group one focus-area fishbone poster to work on, along with 4-5 different color pens. Tell them to color code questions under each factor and across factors using one color per cluster. Tell them to number or label the clusters in some way to further distinguish them. Tell staff to try to cluster questions under the three prioritized factors for the focus areas. Ask if there are any questions. Give groups about 15-20 minutes to accomplish this.

Note: *If there is only one focus area,* the facilitator should lead the discussion with the recorder documenting the information on the fishbone poster.

* (5 minutes) **Closure:** After this is completed, tell the staff that the next step is for the leadership team to take the information generated and prioritized today, and create an investigation plan. This plan will guide the further data collection that will uncover what is impacting student achievement. This is the next step in the process of identifying student learning issues and determining ways to address them. Tell participants when they will meet next as a staff and what they might expect to get from the leadership team.

67

PLANNING THE INVESTIGATION: UNDERSTANDING OUR FOCUS POPULATION AND FACTORS THAT IMPACT STUDENT ACHIEVEMENT

Purpose and Objectives

Without data, staff questions about possible reasons or explanations for a school's student achievement remain unanswered. Planning how and when to gather and use data to answer questions and inform decisions about improvement efforts makes it more likely that the resulting school plan will be tailored to, and effective for, the school.

The purpose of this activity is to design an investigation that will determine how and to what extent the factors identified in Activity 3.2 influence student achievement in the school. The objectives of this activity are to help participants

* develop an understanding of a systematic process for investigating issues related to achievement and school improvement, and

* clarify the questions to be addressed in the investigation, determine the appropriate data needed to answer the questions, and develop strategies for collecting and organizing investigation results.

Background for Facilitators

Rationale

Conducting an investigation into root causes of student achievement is a critical and time-consuming task. Many schools skip this step, moving directly to conclusions about the reasons for their student achievement after only a cursory discussion of the factors that influence it. Doing so makes it much too easy to select programs, strategies, and practices based on *assumed* needs rather than actual needs. To reverse this trend, school teams need to understand how to plan an investigation and collect and organize different types of data.

In this activity, the facilitator engages school teams in a process to help them organize and conduct a focused investigation of factors affecting their student achievement. This activity is appropriate after schools have analyzed their student achievement results and raised questions or offered hunches about why their student achievement is as it is. These questions or hunches should be investigated *before* a school tries to determine school improvement strategies. The issues to be investigated may come from general questions and/or hunches that arose when schools analyzed their achievement results in Activity 2.2, or they may have arisen from discussions in Activity 3.2.

It isn't necessary to have the entire staff participate in this planning, and doing so would consume valuable time better used for other purposes. However, in planning the investigation, the leadership or data team should consider what role other staff members can take in the investigation and development of the school plan. Consider developing a task force for each focus area. All staff could be involved to some degree in one or the other of the task forces, but could play more limited or more extensive roles depending on their time, interest, and level of expertise in the inquiry method. For example, you might ask someone who works especially well with parents and students to help conduct a focus group related to one of the focus areas, but have someone else with stronger analytic skills analyze the data yielded from the focus group. Remember, the more staff that are meaningfully involved in the inquiry process, the more ownership there will be for the outcome.

Source

The activity was developed by WestEd facilitators.

Uses

This activity is designed for use with the school leadership team, data team, leaders of focus area task forces, and/or other school change leaders. Individuals from any or all of these groups will plan the investigation into factors that impact student achievement. They are referred to in the instructions as "Focus Area Teams."

> **Note:** Some data collection tools are provided as tools in this module. If the school (or district) doesn't have tools for investigating particular questions, these tools are available for your use.

Activity Directions

Materials

⇨ Overhead 3.3-1: Challenges in Using Data

⇨ Handout 3.3-1: Data Collection Methods for the Types of Data

⇨ Handout 3.3-2: Digging Deeper Data Tools

⇨ Handout 3.3-3: Sample Investigation Plans (4 pages)

⇨ Overhead 3.3-2: Sample Investigation Plans (4 pages)

⇨ Template 3.3-1: Investigation Plan

⇨ School results from Activities 2.2, 3.2, or any other student achievement analysis activity

⇨ Overhead (to be created by the facilitator) identifying focus areas and the task force leader and members for each one

Time Required

Approximately 2.5 hours

Directions for Facilitators

✳ Before the Activity:

— As described in the Rationale, we recommend that the factor investigations be conducted by focus area task forces. For this activity, in which the factor investigations are *planned*, you'll need to know who will be on these task forces because you will be selecting a subset of each one to engage in the planning. The smaller planning groups are referred to in the directions as the "Focus Area Team."

— Begin by appointing a person to lead the task force for each focus area, then assign staff to focus area task forces. Try to assign one data "expert" to each focus area task force. Staff may have different levels of involvement with their respective task force but all should be associated with one in order to support ownership of the investigation and the results. Create an overhead identifying the focus areas along with the leader and members of each task force.

— From each task force, select a few people to participate in this planning activity. Minimally, include the task force leader and the data expert. Depending on the school's context, it may be advantageous to invite teachers who have the interest and time to join in this activity.

— For each focus area, create an Investigation Plan form using Template 3.3-1 (Investigation Plan) and fill in all known information. For guidance, review Handout 3.3-3 (Sample Investigation Plans). Write the focus area as the title of the form. Fill in the Focus-Area Data Summary from Activity 2.2. In the left column, write the factors and related questions that were identified, developed, and prioritized in Activity 3.2. Arrange the questions in the clusters identified in 3.2, from general to more specific. These questions drive the investigation about how various factors may be affecting student achievement, which, in turn, leads to the identification of effective practices to improve student learning.

— Next, under the heading Characteristics of Focus Population, write specific student-population or program questions identified in Activity 2.2 or Activity 3.2. These questions are related to gaining a deeper understanding of particular groups of students or of students who demonstrate unique patterns of student achievement (e.g., ELL students, special education students). The purpose of these questions is to focus in on the particular students who need assistance so that effective practices with that particular population can be identified and/or the exact student group in need of additional assistance is identified. Questions may be about course enrollment, attendance, or discipline, for example. This heading — Characteristics of Focus Population — also encompasses questions about the impact of programs on students (e.g., high school algebra II students meeting or exceeding the standard compared to high school general math students meeting or exceeding the standard). These types of questions require a further disaggregation of student achievement data than what may be provided on state or district reports. If none of these questions were generated in the previous activities, they don't have to be included.

— For each focus area, make a transparency and enough copies of the partially completed Investigation Plan to hand out for small group work. Have some blank copies of the Investigation Plan template available or provide it electronically on laptops.

— Review Overhead 3.3-2/Handout 3.3-3 (Sample Investigation Plans) and decide which of the two examples (i.e., Language Arts, Math Achievement of Minority Students) is most closely related to the factors the task forces will investigate. Make handouts for investigation groups to refer to when developing their plans.

— Invite the district and school data teams or other data experts to participate to help identify or discuss valid and reliable data sources available to the school, answer questions, and advise the teams when they are deciding what data to collect. For more information about data teams, see Activity 1.9. Invite the data "keepers" in the school, such as the special program coordinators who work with data and other data-oriented staff.

— Review Activity 1.10 (Types of Data and Collection Methods), Activity 1.11 (Validity and the Data-Driven Decision-Making Process), and Handout 3.3-1 (Data Collection Methods for the Types of Data). Make copies of any overheads or handouts from the other activities that you think will be useful.

— Have at hand the school's data inventory showing what data are available, who has them, where they are located, and the format. (For information about school data inventories, see Activity 1.12.)

Introducing the Systematic Process for Planning an Investigation (10 minutes)

✱ (5 minutes) Present a rationale for using a systematic investigation process. Mention that investigating issues using data can take time, but without adequate planning the data collection may not get done or inappropriate data might be collected. Using Overhead 3.3-1 (Challenges in Using Data), talk about these challenges. Ask participants to share successful or challenging data experiences. Avoid getting bogged down in negative experiences.

✱ (5 minutes) Introduce the investigation planning form and process. Show the overhead of one of the partially completed focus area investigation plans created in advance from Template 3.3-1 (Investigation Plan), and orient the group to the process by referring them to the columns, from left to right. Explain where the information that is already filled in came from. Explain that in this activity they will complete the investigation plan for their respective focus areas.

Determining the Data Needed, Data Collection Plan, and Data Analyses (about 2 hours)

✱ (50 minutes) Working focus area by focus area, participants will identify the sources of data for each specific question and write them in the Data Sources/Tool column on the overhead of the focus area Investigation Plan.

— (10 minutes, entire group) Begin by familiarizing the participants with the various types and sources of data that may be appropriate to collect with respect to their questions. Use Handouts 3.3-1 (Data Collection Methods for the Types of Data) and 3.3-2 (Digging Deeper Data Tools). Hand out copies of the example you have chosen from Handout 3.3-3 (Sample Investigation Plans) and have participants look at the various kinds of data in the Data Sources/Tools column. Give people time to review the handouts.

— (5 minutes, entire group) Talk with participants about the validity and reliability of the data they decide to collect for each question they are addressing. See Activity 1.11 for more information and ideas about how to talk about the validity and reliability of data. If needed, use Overhead 1.11-4/Handout 1.11-1 (Validity and the Data-Driven Decision-

Making Process). Remind participants that if data are not "aligned" with the question they are intended to answer, they will provide information that may be erroneous, misleading, or simply not useful.

— (5 minutes, entire group) Tell the participants that triangulation of data is key. Explain that in most cases it is important to gather data from a variety of sources. Use Overhead 3.3-2 (Sample Investigation Plans), focusing on the example you have chosen, and describe how to get a mix of data types to reveal a more complete picture of a factor. Explain that self-reported data (e.g., from interviews, focus groups, and surveys that ask people to report what they are doing) provide a subjective view of what is going on. This view needs to be corroborated with *evidence*. For example, if you were trying to find out the degree to which teachers are using a new reading curriculum, you could ask them. But to confirm that what they report is what actually is happening, you would need to follow up with observation and collection of lesson plans and/or student work. The only instance in which you would not need to corroborate self-reported data is if your objective was to understand how people *perceive* what is going on (e.g., if you wanted to know how students felt about a school schedule change).

— (30 minutes, focus area teams) Have team members decide what data sources they will use to answer the questions under each factor. Remind them of the importance of triangulating data and that it is also important to choose a valid data source that will provide information to address their question. Tell them to write the data sources for the group of questions under the factor in the appropriate column on the planning form. Try to select data sources that will provide data for all of the questions under the factor. Circulate around the room monitoring how well each data source addresses the specific questions to be investigated. Invited data experts should work with focus area teams to help them with this work.

✱ (20-30 minutes, whole group and focus area teams) After 30 minutes, or when it appears the focus area teams have determined data sources and tools, call the entire group back together. Participants will now determine the data analyses and the outcome information needed to answer the questions. The data experts will have a major role in providing technical assistance in this segment. Have participants review the data analysis descriptions in the sample investigation plan you have chosen (from Handout 3.3-3: Sample Investigation Plans) to gain an understanding of how to analyze different types of data. If appropriate, participants should also identify the results of the statistical analyses (e.g., the number and/or percent of students, or the average (mean) for a disaggregated group).

Tell participants that although it is possible to do a statistical analysis of *qualitative* data (e.g., interview, focus group), doing so is not the primary purpose of collecting this type of data. The main purpose of collecting qualitative data is to identify patterns and themes and other information that provides insight into a particular issue. It is a means to "get under the numbers." As part of the analysis, the percentage of people who provide a similar response is recorded as frequencies and percentages. Note: See Tool 3.3d (Handling Messy Data) for a detailed process to use in analyzing interview and focus-group data.

Give teams 10 to 20 minutes to complete the Outcome Information column. Circulate through the room to make sure they are filling in this section correctly.

✱ (10-15 minutes, focus area teams) Participants will determine the status of the data and the data analyses. Distribute and orient groups to the school/district data inventory (see Before the

Activity) and remind them of Handouts 3.3-1 (Data Collection Methods for the Types of Data) and 3.3-2 (Digging Deeper Data Tools). Tell the groups to determine if the data they need for each question are already available in the school or district. Tell them that if the data for a specific question are not available, they should review the data tools in Handout 3.3-2 to see if they are appropriate for addressing the specific question. If not, the data team may need to search for other tools or data after this work session. Let them know that if they do then find the data they need, they should check to see if the desired analysis is also available (e.g., the district teacher survey tallied with percentages for each response).

✱ (10 minutes, focus area teams) Next, have each team decide when to and who will collect, analyze, and report the data. Explain that they must find out how frequently (e.g., monthly, quarterly, annually) data are collected, the dates for obtaining data, and how many of these data are available for analysis. Some data may be already collected on a regular basis. Have teams find out when they are collected and who gets the data; identify the people responsible for collecting, analyzing, and reporting the data; and consider including other appropriate teachers and staff in the data collection and analysis process.

✱ (15-20 minutes, entire group) Talk about how the data will be collected and analyzed. The objective is for focus area team members to get a clear picture of what data collection and analysis for their particular focus area will entail and whether there is overlap with other focus areas. For example, the classroom observation form provided in Tool 3.3b (Classroom Instruction Snapshots) has a summary sheet. If two focus area groups are using this tool to collect data, have them study it together and figure out if their timelines for observation are aligned. If several teams want to conduct interviews or focus groups, have them look at Tool 3.3d (Handling Messy Data). Advise the groups that need interview or focus-group data to make a list of questions that cut across their focus areas so that one interview and/or focus group will suffice for collecting the data sought by multiple groups. For those needing further disaggregation of student achievement data, refer them to activities 2.1 (Analyzing Tables and Graphs to Create Data Statements) and 2.2 (Analyzing Data Statements to Create Focus Area Summaries) for ways to tabulate and analyze their data. Some data will take longer both to collect and to analyze. For example, interview and focus-group data must be transcribed, read multiple times, coded, and tabulated. This is more labor intensive than finding test scores for a particular group of students.

✱ (20 minutes) **Closure:** Tell focus area teams that the investigation plans will be reviewed for overlap. Let participants know that to be prepared for Activity 3.4, they must

— collect any disaggregated student data as outlined in the investigation plan,

— conduct any interviews or focus groups and have the data transcribed and coded,

— administer any surveys and have frequencies and percentages for each question or other analysis as appropriate (i.e., subscales),

— conduct any classroom observations and tabulate data, and

— collect any documents (e.g., lesson plans, student work, professional development plans) and have a short description summarizing what they show.

Make sure team members know when the investigations should be complete and their next meeting date.

Briefly discuss what information needs to be shared with the entire staff or school community (e.g., parent survey is forthcoming, need volunteers for focus groups, overall timeline for completion).

Note: Preparing for Investigation. After the planning session, coordinate the data collection for focus groups or interviews. Either collect the questions generated during this session and compile them into one interview protocol or one set of focus-group questions or meet with the focus area team leaders at a later date to collect questions. Similar steps should be taken for any common data sources that will be used (e.g., classroom observations, collection and review of lesson plans, course enrollment data). Work with focus area team leaders to help them plan and run the interviews and focus groups and arrange for the data to be transcribed. In addition, follow up with each focus area task force to make sure members are able to get the data they need, which could entail, for example, making sure they have release time to conduct classroom observations.

75

ANALYZING AND DESCRIBING FACTOR INVESTIGATION

Purpose and Objectives

Analyzing the data from investigations is often the exciting part of the digging deeper process. It is a time to examine the information that answers the questions and addresses the hunches of the school leadership team, faculty and staff. It is a time to make meaning of the results and start thinking about how to use the findings to decide on relevant school improvement strategies. The objectives of this activity are to help focus area task forces

* analyze the results of their investigations, and

* write the findings as descriptive statements that are objective, understandable, and useful.

Background for Facilitators

Rationale

Task forces for each focus area have expended much energy to gather and organize data from a variety of sources to research the impact of different factors on student achievement. The careful process outlined in this activity helps participants create objective data statements to bring to the full staff.

The data from focus groups, classroom observations, surveys, interviews, enrollment figures, and other sources can be even more challenging to organize, display, and analyze than student achievement data. Yet these data help schools go behind the student achievement data and discover root causes for student achievement challenges. This is a crucial step that, if done rigorously, will lead to the identification of the specific needs that the school must address in order to increase student achievement.

Source

The activity and tools were developed by WestEd facilitators.

Uses

This activity is designed for use with the leadership team, the data team, focus area task forces, or a combination of these groups. This activity is designed to be conducted after all the data specified in focus area investigation plans have been collected. Here, the full task forces or focus area teams that planned the investigation into factors affecting student achievement will now complete the analysis and write data statements. The next step, interpreting and determining the identified needs, occurs in Activity 3.5 and involves the entire staff.

Activity Directions

Materials

⇨ Handout 3.4-1: Investigation Results Examples (4 pages)

⇨ Handout 3.4-2: Guidelines for Writing Statements of Results and Findings

⇨ Handout 3.4-3: Classroom Instruction Snapshots — Example of School Summary Report (2 pages)

⇨ Handout 3.4-4: Procedures for Analyzing Investigation Results

⇨ Template 3.4-1: Investigation Results

⇨ Appropriate data as outlined in the focus area investigation plans (see below in facilitator's directions)

⇨ Highlighters, sticky notes, chart paper

Time Required

Approximately 2 hours

Directions for Facilitators

✱ **Before the Activity:**

— Ask the leaders of whichever teams have conducted the focus area research to bring the necessary copies of the following, as outlined in their respective investigation plan:

- *disaggregated student data as outlined in the investigation plan,*

- *transcripts of interviews or focus groups,*

- *frequencies and percentages for survey questions or other survey analysis as appropriate (e.g., subscales),*

- *tabulated data from classroom observations, and*

- *relevant documents (e.g., lesson plans, student work, professional development plans).*

— Meet with the team leaders to review the data they collected, ensuring that it is accurate and appropriately prepared for analysis. Have them discuss how to organize their teams to complete the activity. If there are multiple factors with multiple questions, it may be advisable to have task force or focus area team members work in pairs on a particular factor. Work should be distributed so that each pair has an equal amount of simple and complex analysis to complete. For example, no one pair should do all of the focus group or interview analysis. Some thought should also be given to how team members are paired and what data they analyze. The goal is to ensure that each pair has the technical skills to complete the needed analysis.

— Either you as the facilitator or the focus area team leaders should begin filling out an Investigation Results form (Template 3.4-1 [Investigation Results]) for each focus area, writing in the focus area, the factors, and the corresponding questions and data sources.

✳ (5-10 minutes) Tell participants that the data related to the factors influencing student achievement have been collected and that today's task is to analyze them and write corresponding data statements.

Refer the group to Handout 3.4-1 (Investigation Results Examples). Tell them that by the end of the session they will have completed their own Investigation results forms for each focus area. Explain that the next step after that will be to share the information on these forms with the entire faculty and jointly determine identified needs for each focus area.

✳ (25-30 minutes) As a group, study the data statements in the Results/Findings column of Handout 3.4-1 (Investigation Results Examples). Using Handout 3.4-2 (Guidelines for Writing Statements of Results and Findings), talk about the elements of a good data statement.

Review writing data statements. Remind participants that they did a similar activity in 2.1 and explain that in this activity they will be using different types of data that, at times, may make it more challenging to write a data statement. Explain that the intent here is to show how data statements (such as the Statements of Results and Findings on Handout 3.4-1 [Investigation Results Examples]) are derived from data sources (such as the observation items on Handout 3.4-3 [Classroom Instruction Snapshots — Example of School Summary Report]). Have participants review the data on the Classroom Instruction Snapshot. Then refer them to the Language Arts example on pages 1-3 of Handout 3.4-1 (Investigation Results Examples), pointing specifically to the second question on page 1: "What research-based instructional practices (including differentiated instruction) do teachers use and how often?" Follow the script below to model how they can think about the data and come up with statements:

> *Okay, this focus area is Language Arts, and the question asks to what degree are teachers using research-based instructional strategies, including differentiated instruction.*
>
> *The classroom observation tool (Tool 3.3b [Classroom Instruction Snapshots]) provides data to answer this question. The data are tallied in this form. Line 13 gives information about research-based strategies. Line 2 says that 80 percent of teachers used some type of research-based strategy. It also shows that only 30 percent used strategies to generate higher-order thinking skills. So let me write a data statement about that information:* Evidence from classroom observations of 20 teachers during Language Arts shows that 80 percent of the 20 teachers used some strategy.
>
> *Let me see if I have all the information I need in this statement. Looking at* Guidelines for Writing Statements of Results and Findings, *I ask myself: Are the facts stated objectively? Is the statement short and clear, written in everyday language? Is it understandable standing alone? Are there relevant numerical data? I think it meets all of those criteria.*

Ask for a volunteer to think about and write a data statement about your own school's data to add to one of the focus area results forms (from Template 3.4-1 [Investigation Results]) that was partially completed in advance for this activity. If possible, use data from a focus group or interview to give participants an opportunity to describe data that are not easily quantifiable. Record the volunteer's data statement on chart paper, prompting him or her with questions to ensure that the statement is as complete as possible. Make sure that teacher anonymity has been protected. When the statement is completed, have participants, as a group, check it against *Guidelines for Writing Statements of Results and Findings*.

79

Ask if there are any questions.

Next, have participants work in pairs to write a statement about an agreed-upon portion of the school data. Have them write their data statements on scratch paper and ask them to check their completed statements against the guidelines.

Ask for a volunteer pair to read their statement. Record the statement on a piece of chart paper. Then lead the staff through the guidelines to evaluate the statement, correcting it if necessary. Repeat the process with additional statements volunteered by the pair until participants feel comfortable with writing and evaluating data statements.

Point participants to the Insights column on Handout 3.4-1 (Investigation Results Examples). Review the statements in that column, and explain that on their own investigation results forms participants might use this column for a number of different kinds of statements. It might include a statement justifying why a particular data statement was included even if it is not directly related to one of the questions. It also might include a statement about a pattern found in the data that does not directly relate to the question but is nonetheless relevant. This column is also a place to put any questions that arise during the data analysis.

(40-60 minutes, focus area teams) Analyze investigation results, using the data to answer the specific investigation questions that were developed earlier. Have the groups follow the instructions in Handout 3.4-4 (Procedures for Analyzing Investigation Results). As they work, circulate among them and check to make sure they are writing objective data statements.

✳ **Closure:** Collect the data statements. Thank participants for their hard work and attention to detail during the investigation. Explain that in the next step the full staff will summarize the findings and determine identified needs.

Note: After this meeting, the school leadership team and/or the data team should review the investigation results for all of the focus area groups and determine if the data statements are an accurate representation of the data and that anonymity has been protected.

SUMMARIZING INVESTIGATION FINDINGS AND DETERMINING IDENTIFIED NEEDS

Purpose and Objectives

At this point, data from multiple sources have been collected and analyzed to understand what factors are impacting student achievement, as well as specifics about the target population. In a previous activity, data statements were created to answer questions focused on understanding these two areas. In this activity, the entire staff will

* review and write summaries of data statements within and across factors for each focus area, and

* determine identified needs for each focus area.

Background for Facilitators

Rationale

In Part 1 of this activity, participants will summarize the data from previous investigations looking for relationships, patterns, and trends among factors affecting student achievement. Summarizing investigation findings is an important activity for a number of reasons. This is a time for staff to develop a deeper understanding of how the factors influence their student achievement. They'll need this foundation as they move further in the planning cycle. The activities in Part 1 help schools transition from the inquiry and needs assessment phase into setting achievement goals and selecting practices (e.g., programs, strategies) to address identified needs. It is especially important because until this point in the investigation, a lot of data work has been done by small groups of people. Now, the full staff needs time to study and understand the findings across data sources before moving on. Without this time to review the data and make sense of them, it is unlikely that the staff will have ownership of the practices selected for the plan as they move through the planning and implementation phases.

Part 2 of the activity builds on the work of Part 1. Using their data summaries, staff begin analyzing and interpreting the data to determine identified needs. The identified needs are the barriers to student achievement that will drive the selection of practices to be included in the school plan.

Source

This activity was developed by WestEd facilitators.

Uses

This activity is designed for use with the full staff.

Activity Directions

Materials

⇨ Overhead 3.5-1: Some Factors That Influence Student Achievement

⇨ Handout 3.5-1: Procedures for Writing Summaries and Determining Identified Needs (2 pages)

⇨ Overhead 3.5-2: Procedures for Writing Summaries and Determining Identified Needs (2 pages)

⇨ Handout 3.5-2: Investigation Results Examples (4 pages)

⇨ Overhead 3.5-3: Investigation Results Examples (4 pages)

⇨ Overhead 3.5-4: Guidelines for Writing Statements of Results and Findings

⇨ Overhead 3.5-5: Determining Identified Needs Example (3 pages)

⇨ Handout 3.5-3: Determining Identified Needs Example (3 pages)

⇨ Overhead 3.5-6: Focus Area Fishbone Chart for Identified Needs: Language Arts Example

⇨ Handout 3.5-4: Assessing Identified Needs: Some Questions to Ask

⇨ Overhead 3.5-7: Refining, Combining, and/or Reducing the Number of Identified Needs

⇨ Template 3.5-1: Determining Identified Needs

⇨ Template 3.5-2: Focus Area Fishbone Chart for Identified Needs

⇨ Investigation Results for each focus areas from Activity 3.4

⇨ Chart paper, markers, large sticky notes or sentence strips, highlighters

Time Required

Approximately 4.25 hours: 2 hours for Part 1 and 2.25 hours for Part 2

Directions for Facilitators

✳ **Before the Activity:**

— Meet with the school leadership or data team or leaders of the focus area task forces to plan the strategies, procedures, and room set-up for this activity, as well as what roles the team members will play.

— Review the data statements created in Activity 3.4 for accuracy and revise if necessary.

— Use Template 3.5-1 (Determining Identified Needs) to create a Determining Identified Needs form for each focus area. For each one, write in the focus area (e.g., language arts, math, ELL), the factor (i.e., element that affects student learning, such as instruction, curriculum, or professional development) and the investigation questions (i.e., questions derived in Activity 3.2 from hunches about the school's student achievement). Make a poster for each factor group (i.e., the small group that will write summaries for each of the factors — see next bullet) that has all the headings from the Determining Identified Needs form. Consider having each factor group work with a laptop and fill in their form electronically in addition to using the posters. Otherwise, the form is not used until after the activity is completed to record what has been generated on the posters. For each focus area, use Template 3.5-2 (Focus Area Fishbone Chart for Identified Needs) to make a fishbone poster for combining and prioritizing identified needs at the end of Part 2. Post them around the room for later use.

— Assign the staff to small groups for each factor in each focus area. If a factor has more than one cluster of investigation questions, as in the language arts example on Overhead 3.5-5 (Determining Identified Needs Example), you might make separate groups depending on the number of staff. Make sure that staff involved in writing data statements in Activity 3.4 are spread among the factor groups rather than kept together as one group. Use these staff members as facilitators for the small groups so the person leading each small group understands the investigation to date. If more than one focus area is being addressed in this activity, select a focus area facilitator who will help focus area groups combine and prioritize identified needs at the end of Part 2. If only one focus area is being addressed, the facilitator for the entire activity can lead the discussion.

— Based on the number of focus areas and the amount of data to be reviewed, decide if the activity will be completed in one or two sessions. Part 1 (Writing Summaries) and Part 2 (Determining Identified Needs) could be done in one session or split into two sessions. It is also possible that a separate session that includes Parts 1 and 2 could be conducted for each focus area.

Make enough copies for the small groups of the completed Investigation Results form for each focus area from Activity 3.4.

Make sure that your copies of Handout 3.5-3 (Determining Identified Needs Example) have the Identified Needs column left blank.

— Meet with the small group facilitators to make sure they understand the process and their role in the activity. Go over the instructions in Handout 3.5-1 (Procedures for Writing Summaries and Determining Identified Needs). Answer any questions they may have. If more than one focus area will be addressed during the activity, meet with the facilitators for the focus area groups at the end of Part 2. Go over their role in combining and prioritizing identified needs.

Provide Overview of Process

Seat staff in their pre-assigned factor groups. Each group should have a pre-assigned facilitator and should select a recorder.

✱ (5 minutes, whole group) Using Overhead 3.5-1 (Some Factors That Influence Student Achievement), remind participants of the work they have already done generating hunches and developing questions related to these factors for each focus area. Describe the planning and data collection process; call upon individuals who were involved in the process to help explain the steps. State that this activity will be the culmination of the investigation phase and will lead to the planning phase.

Pass out Handout 3.5-1 (Procedures for Writing Summaries and Determining Identified Needs). Using the handout and corresponding Overhead 3.5-2, explain that in Part 1, participants will review and summarize the data statements for each factor under the focus areas and will create summary statements. Explain that Part 2 builds on the work of Part 1. (Tell them if Part 2 will be conducted in a separate session) Tell participants that, using their data summaries, they will begin analyzing and interpreting the data to determine identified needs. The identified needs reflect the elements that must be in place to improve student achievement. These needs will drive the selection of practices (e.g., programs, strategies) to be included in the school plan.

Part 1: Writing Factor Summaries (2 hours)

❋ (5 minutes, whole group) **Orientation:** Tell participants that the goal for Part 1 is to write a summary of key data points for each factor in each focus area. Tell them you will model the process using data from a fictitious language arts investigation. Pass out Handout 3.5-2 (Investigation Results Examples). Use corresponding Overhead 3.5-3 to orient participants to the organization of the results. Point out *focus area*, *factor*, and *clusters of investigation questions*. In the example, show how separate clusters of questions may exist under a single factor (e.g., Strategies and Standards under Instruction). Show how the *data statements* are organized by *data sources*. Point out the *Insights* column and explain that this is where interesting observations or additional questions were placed when the focus area teams were writing the data statements.

Tell participants that first they will review the results and findings from various data sources. Then they will learn how to write a summary for each data source and, finally, they will practice writing a summary across data sources for each factor or cluster of questions under a factor. Tell them that after they have reviewed these areas, they will do the same thing working with their own data.

❋ (10 minutes, whole group) Put up the first page of Overhead 3.5-3 (Investigation Results Examples). Focus attention on the data statements for each data source. Remind participants of when they wrote data summaries from their student achievement data. Put up Overhead 3.5-4 (Guidelines for Writing Statements of Results and Findings). Using the criteria, point out how the data statements are descriptive, not interpretive. Explain that in writing summaries, participants will maintain this descriptive stance until in Part 2 when they actually identify needs.

Return to the first page of Overhead 3.5-3 (Investigation Results Example) and refer participants to the corresponding handout. Tell them they will have 5 minutes to read the data statements for the first factor, Instruction, with the question clusters, Strategies and Standards. Tell them to think about which statements they would include in a summary *for each data source*. Tell them to also look at the Insights column for additional statements that might be included in a summary. Suggest using a highlighter as they read to underline the statements or portions of statements they believe should be included for each data source under each factor. Refer them to Handout 3.5-1 (Procedures for Writing Summaries and Determining Identified Needs), steps 1-3 under Data Source Summaries, for the instructions. Tell them that you will go over these instructions in more detail soon. If they finish reading and underlining early, ask them to discuss their thoughts with their table groups.

❋ (12 minutes, whole group) Put up the first page of Overhead 3.5-5 (Determining Identified Needs Example) *with only the data-source summaries visible*. Ask participants to share which data statements they would have selected to include in a summary by data source for each sub-factor (Strategies and Standards) in the example. Explain how data statements were turned into summaries, noting that 1) there is sufficient detail in the summaries to trace back to the original data statements; 2) summaries respond directly to the investigation questions; and 3) summaries, like the data statements, are descriptive, not interpretive.

Tell participants not to ignore the Insights column. After they complete their data-source summaries, tell participants that each factor group should review the Insights column to see if this information should be included. Use Overhead 3.5-5 (Determining Identified Needs Example) to show how the insights were included in the data-source summaries.

Tell participants that when they look at their own data they will be responsible for a data source and will be writing statements on sentence strips to form their summaries for the data source they have been looking at. Direct participants to Handout 3.5-1 (Procedures for Writing Summaries and Determining Identified Needs) and go over the directions.

✳ (15 minutes, whole group and factor groups) Put up the first page of Overhead 3.5-5 (Determining Identified Needs Example) with only the data-source summaries visible. Explain that the next step is to write a summary across data sources for each factor or, in this case, create summaries for the question clusters (Strategies and Standards). Tell participants that in table groups they will read the data-source summaries on the overhead and merge them, including any insights, into their own cross-data-source factor summary for each of the question clusters.

For instructions, again direct participants to Handout 3.5-1 (Procedures for Writing Summaries and Determining Identified Needs). Tell participants to write their summary on chart paper. Walk around and listen to the different table groups to make sure they understand the task and are moving forward. If the majority of the groups are not able to create the factor summary, do the Strategies summary together and have them do the Standards summary on their own.

✳ (15 minutes, whole group and factor groups) On Overhead 3.5-5 (Determining Identified Needs Example), display both the data-source and cross-data-source factor summaries. Ask participants to compare and discuss at their tables (5 minutes) the similarities and differences between their charted summaries and the summary on the overhead. Discuss the summaries as a whole group, using the participants' summaries or the example on the overhead. Bring up the following:

— Tell participants that there is no single way to write a factor summary. Different versions of a factor summary could be accurate and appropriate if the following three things were true: 1) there was sufficient detail in the summary to be able to trace back to the original data statements; 2) the summary responded directly to the investigation questions; and 3) the summary, like the data statements, was descriptive, not interpretive.

— Describe the importance of triangulation of data. The most important statements to include are often the ones for which you have multiple data sources, preferably three, showing the same thing.

— Tell participants that they will be using the sentence strips from their own data to create the cross-data-source factor summaries. Point this out in the instructions on Overhead 3.5-2 (Procedures for Writing Summaries and Determining Identified Needs).

✳ (45 minutes, factor groups) Give teams their data and factor assignments. Distribute Handout 3.5-3 (Determining Identified Needs Example) for teams' reference (Note: Make sure you are using the handout with the Identified Needs column left blank.) Using Handout 3.5-1 (Procedures for Writing Summaries and Determining Identified Needs) and corresponding Overhead 3.5-2, review the process for, first, writing the data-source summaries for each factor or each question cluster under a factor and, second, creating the cross-data-source factor summaries. Check with the factor group facilitators to ensure that they understand their role in leading the team through the process as described on the procedures handout. Circulate among the groups. Observe and work with each group to make sure they are accurately summarizing the investigation findings for each factor.

85

✳ (15 minutes, whole group) When table groups are done, have a few teams share their data-source summaries and read their cross-data-source factor summaries. Ask for comments or questions.

✳ (5 minutes) **Closure for Part 1:** Explain to participants that in creating a summary of investigation results for their factor, they have gotten to know very well the evidence describing the role of that factor in their student achievement. Explain that in the next part of the activity, they will use these summaries to look within and across factors to determine the identified needs of the school in each focus area. (Note: if Part 2, Determining Identified Needs, is to be done as a separate activity, you might want to extend this closure to include a gallery walk, then discuss as a group.)

Part 2: Determining Identified Needs (2.25 hours)

Seat staff in their pre-assigned factor groups. Each group should have a pre-assigned facilitator and should select a recorder. If you intend to address more than one focus area in this activity, have a facilitator ready for each one.

> Note: If Part 2 is being done as a separate session, review with the participants the examples of focus area, factor, data-source summaries, and the process for creating the cross-data-source factor summaries, using Handout 3.5-1 (Procedures for Writing Summaries and Determining Identified Needs) and corresponding Overhead 3.5-2.

✳ (5 minutes, factor groups) **Orientation:** Explain the concept and importance of identified needs. Cover the following:

— *Identified needs are the root causes of low student achievement.* They are determined through the school's research into the factors such as curriculum, instruction, and professional development. The actions, strategies, or practices that are put in the school plan will be chosen because they have been shown to address the identified needs in schools with a similar context (i.e., similar student population, size, instructional programs, etc). The identified need should be a response to the question, "What is the greatest challenge to student achievement that you see in this summary?"

— *In determining identified needs participants will move from describing to interpreting.* Tell them they will look back to the original questions and hunches to see if the data validate those hunches. An identified need will always have data to back up the statement. If done properly, participants should be able to trace an identified need back to a couple of data sources.

— *Determine identified needs first within factors, then across factors.* There may not be an identified need for every factor. The staff might have had a hunch or question that, when investigated, proves not to be an identified need. Also, it is possible to have more than one identified need for a single factor.

— *Not all identified needs are of equal importance.* The activity will culminate with a grouping or prioritization of the identified needs.

✳ (10 minutes, whole group) **Modeling the Process of Determining Identified Needs.** As a group, look at the Factor Summary column for Collaboration on page 2 of Handout 3.5-3 (Determining Identified Needs Example) and Overhead 3.5-5 with the same name. *Conceal the*

Identified Needs column on the overhead. (That column has been left blank on the handout.)
Refer participants to Handout 3.5-1 (Procedures for Writing Summaries and Determining
Identified Needs) for instructions and for the criteria for the identified needs. Use the following
script as you model the thought process behind determining the identified need for Collaboration,
referring to the overhead as you talk:

> *I see there are three questions about collaboration that prompted our investigation: one
> about how often teachers collaborate, one about what they do when they collaborate,
> and one about how they used classroom assessment data to inform instruction. I want
> to look at the answers to these questions while I consider the question, "What is the
> greatest challenge to student achievement that I see in this summary?"*

> *From the Factor Summary in the center column I see the answers to some of these
> questions. Teachers are collaborating about three hours per month by grade levels.
> This tells me that having time for collaboration isn't a problem, so I'm going to dig a
> little deeper to see how teachers are using their time together.*

> *From the Factor Summary and from the data-source summaries, I can see that really
> only the 3rd grade teachers have common assessments and that is the only grade
> level in which common strategies are discussed and common assessments are
> administered and scored. It seems the other grade levels know how to do this because
> they discuss the data that comes from the district benchmarks and talk about how they
> should change instruction as a result.*

> *I'm starting to see that the challenge is not about the amount of time or a common
> protocol for collaboration, but rather about having common data to talk about so they
> can use their time together effectively. If they had common assessments given more
> frequently than the district benchmarks, they could talk about their instruction and
> ways of differentiating it for different groups of students, especially ELL students. It
> would also help to have a pacing guide that everyone at a grade level stayed pretty
> close to, so that they would have some common curriculum to talk about.*

> *So, I'll write my identified need around collaboration as follows: The lack of common
> assessments and pacing guides limits the ability of teachers to use existing
> collaboration time effectively in discussing student work, ongoing assessments, and
> instructional strategies, especially to support ELL students.*

Tell participants that there are many ways you could have written this identified need but that
the outcome would be roughly equivalent. Using the criteria on Handout 3.5-1 (Procedures for
Writing Summaries and Determining Identified Needs), show how this identified need meets the
criteria: 1) it responds to the original investigation questions; 2) the need can be traced back
to the data sources; 3) effective collaboration is one of the factors we know affects student
achievement; and 4) it isn't just a restatement of the data, but an interpretation that can lead to a
change in practice.

Ask participants to consider why you didn't conclude that there was a need for more
collaboration time or for professional development in how to collaborate. Responses should
focus on how you interpreted the investigation data to see the greatest challenge — teachers
didn't need more time or training in collaboration until they actually had something in common
around which to collaborate. This identified need focuses on the most basic barrier to effective
collaboration and thus student achievement.

87

* (15 minutes, whole group and factor groups) As a group, look at the factor summary for Strategies on page 1 of Handout 3.5-3 (Determining Identified Needs Example) and corresponding Overhead 3.5-5. Tell table groups to use a Think-Pair-Share to determine the identified need in the Strategies summary. Tell them to take 8 minutes to first think by themselves, then talk with a partner, and then, as a table group, discuss the question, "What is the greatest challenge to student achievement that you see in this summary?" Tell participants to make notes in the identified need column of the handout. For instructions and the criteria for the identified needs, refer them to Handout 3.5-1 (Procedures for Writing Summaries and Determining Identified Needs).

After 8 minutes, call the group back together and display the identified need for Strategies on the Overhead 3.5-5 (Determining Identified Needs Example). Discuss the identified need the teams came up with for Strategies. Using Handout 3.5-1 (Procedures for Writing Summaries and Determining Identified Needs) again, review how the identified need in the example meets the criteria.

* (30 minutes, factor groups) **Determining Identified Needs.** Give participants the investigation findings they used and the original charts with data source and factor summaries that they created in Part 1. Tell factor groups that they will now determine an identified need, if there is one, for their factor. Later, they will determine identified needs across factors for a focus area. Recommend a similar procedure to what was used in the example, in which they first think by themselves, then talk with a partner, and then, as a table group, discuss the question, "What is the greatest challenge to student achievement that you see in this summary?" Refer them again to Handout 3.5-1 (Procedures for Writing Summaries and Determining Identified Needs) for instructions and for the criteria for the identified needs. Tell them to write their identified need on the chart paper next to their factor summary when it is complete. Ask recorders in each group to also write their identified need on a sentence strip or large sticky note for later work.

While the factor groups work, circulate and listen to ensure that they are following the instructions and that their discussions are moving them closer to determining the identified need. You may need to bring them back to their original data sources or highlight commonalities in the findings so they stay focused on their factor. It may not take the full time for factor groups to determine their identified need.

Note: The remainder of the activity is written as if more than one focus area is being addressed in the session. If only one focus area is being addressed, modify the directions accordingly.

* (15 minutes, whole group) When each factor group has finished, tell them that they will do a gallery walk to see the other identified needs for other factors in their focus area. Tell them that they will have 10 minutes to see all of the factors and to take notes on common or related needs that they see. Have each group select a person to remain at their chart to explain their summary and identified need. Tell participants that after the gallery walk they will sit in focus area groups instead of factor groups.

Note: Use the gallery walk time to set up for the next portion of the activity, including moving tables and chairs adjacent to the fishbone charts. Touch base with the focus area facilitators identified before the activity and remind them that they will be facilitating the next portion of the activity. Have them stand by their focus area fishbone chart to review the identified needs as they are put on it. Tell the recorders from the factor groups to take the identified need that they wrote on a sentence strip or sticky note and attach it to the appropriate focus area fishbone chart. Review all the identified needs for the different factors and see if there are any that are redundant, could be combined, or are of higher priority than others. If so, note them for later reference in the activity.

After the gallery walk, ask participants to sit by their focus area fishbone poster. Have the people who stayed by the charts during the gallery walk post their charts, with the data-source and factor summaries and identified needs, closer to the related focus area fishbone poster. Once participants are seated near their appropriate fishbone poster, have a brief group discussion about any common or related needs across factors and within focus areas that participants might have noted during the gallery walk.

* (15 minutes, whole group) **Modeling the Process of Refining, Combining, and/or Reducing the Number of Identified Needs**. Remind participants that their goal is to determine for each focus area a *limited* number of identified needs that can be addressed in the school plan. Note that the identified needs they generated are displayed under the corresponding factor on the fishbone chart. Tell participants that having a long list of identified needs is sometimes overwhelming for schools. In trying to address many things at once, attention and efforts may become diffused and the most important things may get lost. Explain that their next task will be to assess which identified needs are pivotal to their improvement efforts. In this last portion of the activity, they will be refining, combining, and/or reducing the number of identified needs with the goal of having three to five well-defined identified needs for each focus area.

Model the process. Using Overhead 3.5-6 (Focus Area Fishbone Chart for Identified Needs: Language Arts Example), remind participants that their work thus far has been based on an example of a fictitious school identifying needs for only a few factors. A real school would actually have a number of factors that had been investigated and probably a long list of identified needs. The fishbone represents the completed work of the fictitious school across five factors. Tell participants to get out Handout 3.5-1 (Procedures for Writing Summaries and Determining Identified Needs) and to look at the instructions for Refining, Combining, and/or Reducing the Number of Identified Needs. Meanwhile, pass out Handout 3.5-4 (Assessing Identified Needs: Some Questions to Ask). Tell participants that you will model some of the process of refining, combining, and/or reducing the number of identified needs for them.

Tell participants to look at the identified need for collaboration and look at the questions on Handout 3.5-4 (Assessing Identified Needs: Some Questions to Ask). Tell them the answer to all the questions for this identified need is *yes*. All teachers are involved in collaboration. Improved instruction will benefit all students, but especially the struggling students. It is obviously focused on the classroom, but any response to this identified need will impact all teachers, all students and the use of instructional materials. Tell participants that this is what they should expect to see in any well-written identified need.

89

Put up Overhead 3.5-7 (Refining, Combining, and/or Reducing the Number of Identified Needs). Point out the existing identified needs for Curriculum. Tell participants that this is an obvious example of two that could be combined. It will lead to a more comprehensive solution when combined, impacting more students, more teachers, and possibly materials other than just the reading series.

Point out the identified needs for Professional Development. Explain that keeping these separate could mean that the ongoing professional development or coaching that ends up in the school plan might not address the professional development needs of the teachers. Keeping them separate raises the risk of having ongoing professional development focused on things with which they really don't need help.

Point out the identified need for the factor Staff Expectations. Explain that this is a very difficult identified need to consider. To have even identified it took courage on the part of the staff. Acknowledge that it is difficult for a staff to admit that a number of them have low expectations for students. Tell them that this is really an identified need about professional development that will help teachers understand what kind of progress they should expect from ELL students. In combining it with the professional development identified need, as shown, they would have to be careful not to lose the point that staff expectations were low.

Refer staff back to Handout 3.5-1 (Procedures for Writing Summaries and Determining Identified Needs), specifically to the instructions for Refining, Combining, and/or Reducing the Number of Identified Needs. Review the directions. Tell staff that what you have modeled is the process they will use and the sort of conversations they will have in their focus area groups, led by their focus area facilitator. Have facilitators identify themselves. Ask if there are any questions. Remind them that the goal is to have three to five well-defined, identified needs for their focus area after a half hour of conversation.

* (30 minutes, focus area groups) Circulate as the groups work. Point out identified needs that you determined during the gallery walk could be combined. Also, point out common or related needs across factors. If they seem to be having difficulty understanding how to combine or refine needs, refer them to Handout 3.5-4 (Assessing Identified Needs: Some Questions to Ask), to Handout 3.5-3 (Determining Identified Needs Example) *without* the identified needs, to Overhead 3.5-5 (Determining Identified Needs Example) *with* the identified needs, or Overhead 3.5-7 (Refining, Combining, and/or Reducing the Number of Identified Needs).

(10 minutes, whole group) When focus area groups are finished or after 30 minutes, whichever comes first, call the whole group back together. Ask each focus area group to share a part of their work that was particularly difficult or changed the way members had been thinking. Point out any commonalities across focus areas you noticed while the groups were working. For example, implementing effective instructional strategies may be a need in both math and language arts.

* (5 minutes, whole group) **Closure:** Publicly recognize the hard work of the staff and different teams who collected and analyzed the data to this point. Explain to staff that this activity represents a turning point in the data-driven decision-making process, completing the investigation phase and beginning the planning phase. Tell participants that someone will record the data source and factor summaries and the related identified needs. These will be shared with the appropriate constituents. Tell participants that as a next step they will begin identifying practices, activities, and programs to directly address their identified needs.

91

Module 4:
Writing Student
Achievement Goals

92

WRITING STUDENT ACHIEVEMENT GOALS

Purpose and Objectives

A good action plan improves a few key areas of student achievement that all stakeholders agree are the priority areas of concern. These priority areas emerge from the needs assessment and the data analysis discussions. In Module 2, the school determined "achievement results or findings" and focus areas based on those findings. In this activity, the school will transform those data statements into annual student achievement goals for each focus area.

Specifically, participants will

* learn the criteria for a student achievement goal,

* practice writing clear and concise student achievement goals, and

* create student achievement goals that address the data statements in the focus areas.

Background for Facilitators

Rationale

Many schools jump directly from the needs assessment to choosing strategies and actions without first identifying desired changes in student achievement or behavior. By not setting specific growth targets, schools sidestep accountability. To ensure that a plan will make a difference for students, a school team must define the achievement target they hope to reach when undertaking specific actions. This activity focuses on student achievement goals, but a school could also have goals related to student behavior, such as improved attendance, decreased discipline referrals, or a higher graduation rate.

Schmoker (1999) warns that schools should only have one or possibly two goals for each focus area such as reading, math or behavior. Schools do not have time to adequately address all possible areas well. Data-driven decision-making means taking focused, targeted action to address identified needs. As a result of this activity, schools will write annual student achievement goals. These goals say that if we, as a school, execute our plan well, at the end of the school year we expect our students to achieve at the specified levels on a particular assessment. The No Child Left Behind (NCLB) legislation mandates that states set annual growth targets in the form of Annual Yearly Progress. The school will want to align its goals with state or federal targets and, at the same time, ensure that it addresses school-specific findings based on grade-level or subject-area data.

Source

This activity was developed by WestEd facilitators.

Reference

Schmoker, M. J. (1999). *Results: The key to continuous school improvement* (2nd Ed.). Alexandria, VA: Association for Supervision and Curriculum Development.

Uses

This activity is appropriate for the full school staff. It should be used after extensive analysis of evidence and student achievement data, but it requires little prior knowledge on the part of most participants. Findings from within and across grade-level and subject-area analyses should be available to participants.

There are many sets of criteria for student achievement goals. All handouts and overheads are designed for one set of criteria. If your school, district, or organization has a different set of criteria, it can easily be substituted on the handouts and overheads.

Activity Directions

Materials

⇨ Handout 4.1-1: Writing Student Achievement Goals

⇨ Overhead 4.1-1: Criteria for a Measurable Student Achievement Goal

⇨ Overhead 4.1-2: Sample Student Achievement Goals

⇨ Handout 4.1-2: Practice Goals Worksheet

⇨ Overhead 4.1-3: Practice Goals Worksheet

⇨ Template 4.1-1: Student Achievement Goals Worksheet

Time Required

Approximately 1.25 hours

Directions for Facilitators

✶ **Before the Activity:** If a different set of criteria for student achievement goals is to be used, revise the handouts and overheads accordingly. Use the data statements from previous analyses of student achievement data and information about target areas for change from Activity 2.2 to fill in the Focus Areas and the Data Statements ahead of time on Template 4.1-1 (Student Achievement Goals Worksheet). Gather information on your state's NCLB Adequate Yearly Progress requirements to share with staff during the activity. Make an overhead and handouts of the partially completed worksheet.

✶ (20 minutes) Begin by explaining that to focus their planning process the staff needs to establish measurable annual goals. Tell participants that when they implement their plan they will also establish interim targets to show they are making progress toward the annual goal. For now, they need to set annual goals in each of their focus areas to address areas of low performance schoolwide or for subgroups of the school population. Pass out Handout 4.1-1 (Writing Student Achievement Goals). Show participants Overhead 4.1-1 (Criteria for a Measurable Student Achievement Goal). Explain each criterion. Emphasize that a goal must be achievable and must also be designed to hold the school accountable for making a significant difference in student achievement. Show the sample student achievement goals on Overhead 4.1-2 (Sample Student Achievement Goals). Describe how each goal meets the criteria. Point out how one of the goals states the degree to which the achievement gap will be closed. Tell participants that if they have identified gaps between subgroups in their data, it will be important to specify how the school will know the performance gaps are closing.

✳ (15 minutes) Ask participants to work in groups to revise the Sample Goals in the left-hand column of Handout 4.1-2 (Practice Goals Worksheet) so they meet the criteria for an achievement goal.

✳ (10 minutes) Using Overhead 4.1-3 (Practice Goals Worksheet), ask participants to report out changes they made and how the changes address the criteria.

✳ (20 minutes) Give participants copies of the partially completed Student Achievement Goals Worksheet (from Template 4.1-1), explaining that they will now use what they have learned to write goals for their own school. Show them the data statements using an overhead of the worksheet and ask participants to work in groups to create a student achievement goal for each of the data statements. Make sure teams have the necessary information for writing goals that meet state or federal accountability requirements.

✳ (10 minutes) Use the overhead of the Student Achievement Goals Worksheet to record the goals the groups have developed. With multiple groups working on the same data statement you may end up with redundant or divergent goals. As a whole group, evaluate the proposed goals and try to reach consensus about a set of goals. Remind participants to evaluate the goals based on the criteria.

✳ (5 minutes) **Closure:** If there is no consensus on the goals after a short discussion, tell participants that a team will review them and will submit a set of revised goals to the full staff. Remind them that once they begin implementing the plan, they will write interim goals so they can judge if they are making adequate progress toward the annual goal and make midterm adjustments to the plan if necessary. Inform participants that the next step will be to begin research to find effective practices that will help students meet the achievement goals.

95

UNDERSTANDING THE ELEMENTS OF SCHOOL CHANGE

Purpose and Objectives

At this point in the change process, school teams have established student achievement goals in each focus area identified in the needs assessment. In this activity, attention turns to exploring how best to meet these goals. This activity presents a research-based framework that will guide school teams in the selection of effective practices. In particular, it will help school teams

* learn about the three key elements of instructional capacity and how these elements work together to leverage change, and

* understand how this framework will guide the search for effective practices to address identified needs.

Background for Facilitators

Rationale

Those involved in school change efforts frequently observe school leaders moving directly from analyzing data to writing a school plan. There is a gap between identifying needs and choosing what practices will be included in the plan in hopes that they will effectively address those needs. Moreover, there is rarely a set of critical questions or decision-making filters in place to guide the *search* for effective practices that will address a school's identified needs. As when they are determining the root causes of a problem, school teams must also engage in a thoughtful process leading up to the selection of effective practices. Drawing on research by Cohen and Ball (1999) and using a school scenario, this activity helps school teams develop a framework for researching their own solutions that focus on improving classroom instruction. Additionally, school teams will learn that interventions are likely to be more effective if they target multiple interactions among the elements of instruction, rather than focusing on just one element in isolation from others.

Source

This activity was developed by WestEd facilitators.

References

Cohen, D. K., & Ball, D. L. (1999). *Instruction, capacity, and improvement* (Consortium for Policy Research in Education Research Report Series, #RR-043). Philadelphia: Consortium for Policy Research in Education. Available at http://www.cpre.org/Publications/rr43.pdf. Last accessed on June 9, 2006.

Uses

This activity is appropriate for use at the beginning of the search for effective practices. It is assumed that the school has identified some key problems, examined underlying factors, and set achievement goals. The activity will set the stage for investigating effective practices to address identified needs. The participants should be those involved in the search for strategies (e.g., focus area task forces, full staff).

Materials

⇨ Handout 4.2-1: Scenario for School Improvement: Collins Middle School

⇨ Overhead 4.2-1: Scenario for School Improvement: Collins Middle School

⇨ Overhead 4.2-2: Reflection Questions for Collins Middle School

⇨ Overhead 4.2-3: Instructional Capacity

⇨ Overhead 4.2-4: Capacity and Interaction

⇨ Handout 4.2-2: Focus on Teachers

⇨ Handout 4.2-3: Focus on Students

⇨ Handout 4.2-4: Focus on Materials

⇨ Handout 4.2-5: Focus on Capacity

⇨ Overhead 4.2-5: Every Intervention

⇨ Overhead projector, chart paper, blank overhead transparencies, overhead pens or markers

Time Required

Approximately 1.25 hours

Directions for Facilitators

✱ **Before the Activity:** Think through the jigsaw portion of this activity based on the number of participants anticipated in the session. The jigsaw portion can be done as a single group if there are relatively few attendees. Also, on an overhead transparency or chart paper create a T-chart with the headings "Experience" and "Outcome."

✱ (5 minutes) Explain to participants that over the next hour they will be thinking deeply about the next steps in the planning process (i.e., researching and selecting effective practices to address the school's identified needs). Explain that, given the time participants have spent identifying the school's needs, they will want to have a thoughtful process for identifying solutions that will influence student achievement.

✱ (5 minutes) Pass out the Handout 4.2-1 (Scenario for School Improvement: Collins Middle School) and ask all participants to read the short scenario.

✱ (10 minutes) Put up Overhead 4.2-2 (Reflection Questions for Collins Middle School) and use the questions to lead a discussion with participants. Have Overhead 4.2-1 (Scenario for School Improvement: Collins Middle School) available to point to specific examples, if necessary.

✱ (10 minutes) Using the final reflection question regarding prior experience, tap into participants' prior experience with a similar endeavor. Using the T-chart with the headings "Experience" and "Outcome," record some of participants' experiences on the overhead or chart paper.

✱ (10 minutes) Put up Overhead 4.2-3 (Instructional Capacity). Make the following points in explaining the Cohen and Ball framework for instructional capacity.

— Cohen and Ball argue that improving instructional capacity requires a focus on some combination of three elements — teachers, students, and materials — and, especially, the interaction between these three elements.

— Interventions are likely to be more effective if they target multiple interactions among more elements of instruction, rather than focusing on one element in isolation from others.

— Interventions need not act directly on all elements — on teachers, students, and materials. Those that work indirectly on all three elements could be more effective than interventions that work directly only on one element.

— Definition: **Teachers:** When talking about teachers, Cohen and Ball emphasize both their intellectual and interpersonal interactions with students. These include teachers' understanding of knowledge; understanding of the content area; awareness of students' knowledge level and ability to relate to the content; repertoire of teaching strategies; and ability to establish the classroom environment.

— Definition: **Students:** When talking about students, Cohen and Ball emphasize that the resources students bring to the classroom influence what teachers can accomplish. These resources include their experience, their prior knowledge, the habits of mind that influence what they attend to, how they interpret things, and their response to both materials and teachers.

— Definition: **Materials:** Cohen and Ball broadly define materials as that with which students engage including texts, problems, tasks and questions.

— Cohen and Ball emphasize that what students and teachers bring to interactions is not fixed. The point is that what students and teachers bring to a situation may be used to enhance learning. This is true of materials as well; what matters is not the material itself, but how it is used by the teacher and the students.

— Point out how the Collins' plan focuses on only one aspect — the students — and does not connect with the teacher, materials, or classroom instruction.

✱ (10 minutes) Using Overhead 4.2-4 (Capacity and Interaction), explain that participant groups will read and discuss one of four excerpts from Cohen and Ball. Organize participants into four groups and distribute the excerpts (Handouts 4.2-2 [Focus on Teachers], 4.2-3 [Focus on Students], 4.2-4 [Focus on Materials], and 4.2-5 [Focus on Capacity], giving a different handout to each group. Ask participants to note or highlight important points as they read. When they have finished, ask the table groups to discuss the important points from their reading and be prepared to report out.

✱ (15 minutes) Put up Overhead 4.2-3 (Instructional Capacity) again. Then have each small group report out to the entire group, identifying its main point. Have participants relate the reading and what they learned to the visual on the overhead. Ask if they believe the interaction of these elements leads to increased student learning. Ask participants to provide examples from their own experience. Reiterate some of the points made when you first introduced the visual. If appropriate, refer back to the T-chart on the overhead or chart paper.

✱ (5 minutes) Put up Overhead 4.2-5 (Every Intervention) and read it aloud. Ask participants to reflect on this idea. Ask them to connect the quote with the previous discussion and to think about how it might influence what they will select as a strategy or program. Ask for volunteers to share their reflections.

99

✳ (10 minutes) **Closure:** Lead a discussion on how participants could use Cohen and Ball's Instructional Capacity framework to focus their search for strategies and/or programs to address their identified needs. Note suggestions on the overhead or on chart paper. Explain that they will use this framework to begin selecting effective practices (including activities and programs) to put into the school plan.

PLANNING FOR INVESTIGATING EFFECTIVE PRACTICES

Purpose and Objectives

The leadership team, expanded with the task force leaders if they are not already members, should carefully map out the process prior to beginning the investigation of potential practices. In this activity the team will

* develop a plan for investigating and adopting effective practices, and

* ensure that the investigation is an inclusive process that will increase ownership of the final decisions about which effective practices to include in the school plan.

Background for Facilitators

Rationale

Selecting effective practices to address identified needs is a critical step in the planning and implementation of the school plan. Effective practices are those things the school will do to reach its student achievement goal; they are the heart of the improvement effort, and all staff must be committed to them. To ensure maximum ownership, careful planning about how the investigation will be conducted must occur with decisions made about who will be involved, how decisions will be made, and on what timeline. This planning should occur prior to starting the investigation.

The central issue in planning the investigation is how to build ownership across the entire staff. Ownership is more than buy-in, which connotes agreement *after* a decision has been made. Ownership occurs when the staff is involved in the decision-making process. This leads to a deeper level of commitment and, therefore, greater support when implementing the plan.

Source

This activity was developed by WestEd facilitators.

Uses

In this activity, the leadership team will make all the necessary decisions about *how* to investigate and choose what practices to include in the school plan.

Materials

⇨ Handout 4.3-1: Investigating Effective Practices Planning Form (2 pages)

⇨ Handout 4.3-2: Who Will Be Involved?

⇨ Handout 4.3-3: Tasks in the Investigation Process (2 pages)

⇨ Overhead 4.3-1: Investigating Effective Practices Planning Form (2 pages)

⇨ Handout 4.3-4: The Timeline

⇨ Copies of activities referred to in the Task column of Handout 4.3-1: Investigating Effective Practices Planning Form

⇨ Copies of the school's roadmap, developed in Activity 1 of the *Change Manager's Handbook*

⇨ Overhead projector, chart paper, overhead pens or markers

Time Required

Approximately 1.5 hours

Directions for Facilitators

✳ **Before the Activity:**

— Make copies of the activities referred to in the Task column of Handout 4.3-1 (Investigating Effective Practices Planning Form), that is, Activities 4.4, 4.5, and 4.6.

— Review Step 1b, beginning on page 62 of the *Change Manager's Handbook,* on fostering ownership for decisions. Make copies of the school's roadmap of activities and tools that was developed using the *Change Manager's Handbook.*

— Obtain and make copies of the school calendar, which should include all external and internal deadlines, scheduled meetings, etc.

(5 minutes) Distribute copies of Handout 4.3-1 (Investigating Effective Practices Planning Form). Also hand out copies of the school's roadmap for reference. Explain how important it is to carefully plan the investigation for effective practices. Tell team members that they must carefully consider what steps to take, who needs to be involved to build ownership for the final decisions, and when investigation participants will complete each step. On the roadmap, point out the initial plan for investigating effective practices. Explain that this plan forms the skeleton of the investigation, but now that the school has established its identified needs and is further along in the inquiry process, a more-detailed plan is necessary. Tell them that as they create an investigation plan specific to their identified needs, they will be balancing the importance of building ownership against the time available to complete the investigation.

(10 minutes) Ask participants to read the information on Handout 4.3-2 (Who Will Be Involved). After they have finished, discuss and write on the chart paper a list of those who need to participate in the investigation.

(20 minutes) Ask participants to spend about 5 minutes reading the information on Handout 4.3-3 (Tasks in the Investigation Process). Tell participants that as they read they should highlight or underline numbered steps in the investigation process. Have the roadmap and copies of the activities that are referenced in the handout available for the participants to review if needed. When reviewing the activities, participants should pay particular attention to Activity 4.5 and the time commitments for each step in the process. Finally, using Overhead 4.3-1 (Investigating Effective Practices Planning Form), lead a brief discussion to ensure that all participants understand each task and what is involved.

(25 minutes) Give participants 5 minutes to read Handout 4.3-4 (The Timeline) and make some notes on their copy of Handout 4.3-1 (Investigating Effective Practices Planning Form). Have available copies of any schedules and timelines with externally imposed deadlines, meeting

schedules, etc. Know how much time is available during staff meetings or other meeting times for the tasks outlined above. After participants have read the timeline passage, work with them to fill in the appropriate timeline for each task, using Overhead 4.3-1 (Investigating Effective Practices Planning Form). Emphasize that their task is to work within the external deadlines and time available to create a process that will build ownership for the practices ultimately chosen to be included in the school plan. Use the calendar of meetings and deadlines to plan. Make sure there is sufficient time for each activity. Revise steps accordingly.

> Note: You may find that the conversations about the timeline and the people involved in the investigation become intertwined. This is to be expected. You may wish to combine the timeline and the "who's involved" segments.

(20 minutes) Tell participants they will now fill in the Who's Involved column of the planning form. Review the list created earlier of individuals or groups to be included. On Overhead 4.3-1 (Investigating Effective Practices Planning Form) add who should conduct or be involved in each of the tasks. Review again the concept of ownership and strongly recommend that all staff be involved in the final decision-making process to cultivate greater ownership.

(10 minutes) **Closure:** When the planning form has been completed, reiterate the importance of having the full staff understand the investigation plan and the rationale behind decisions related to it. Determine a time to share the plan with the staff and decide who will help with that presentation.

GENERATING A LIST OF EFFECTIVE PRACTICES FOR INVESTIGATION

Purpose and Objectives

This activity builds on Cohen and Ball's three elements of the instructional unit — teachers, students, and materials — presented in Activity 4.2. This framework will guide the school's investigation into effective practices. As a result of this activity, participants will

* have a clear understanding of the process to be used for the investigation and final selection of effective practices in each focus area,

* brainstorm and list effective strategies for each focus area in the correct circle(s) of the Venn diagram related to Cohen and Ball's instructional unit, and

* create a list of potential effective practices or programs for further investigation.

Background for Facilitators

Rationale

This activity is designed to help schools avoid the temptation to pick effective strategies simply because it *seems* like they would be good. The goal is to build a sound rationale for researching and ultimately selecting the strategies that will drive the school change process for the next year. Clear links are made to the results of the needs assessment and the elements of Cohen and Ball's framework for increasing instructional capacity (see Activity 4.2). While participants are encouraged to list potential solutions from a variety of sources, only those that make it through the initial filters will be further researched.

It is unlikely that the entire staff will participate in the full investigation. It is more likely that a leadership team or several task forces will be charged with this task. To guide their research, Activity 4.5 includes a list of websites and a recording form. Activity 4.6 will help them in presenting the results of their research to the full staff and reach consensus on which practices will actually be part of the school plan.

Source

This activity was developed by WestEd facilitators.

References

Cohen, D. K., & Ball, D. L. (1999). *Instruction, capacity, and improvement* (Consortium for Policy Research in Education Research Report Series, #RR-043). Philadelphia: Consortium for Policy Research in Education. Available at http://www.cpre.org/Publications/rr43.pdf. Last accessed on June 9, 2006.

Uses

This activity is designed for use with the full staff prior to investigation of effective strategies. Ownership for subsequent school changes will be greater if more people are involved in meaningful ways in the planning process. While not everyone needs to be involved in the actual investigation of effective practices, everyone should contribute to the list of potential practices to investigate.

Materials

⇨ Overhead 4.4-1: Instructional Capacity

⇨ Overhead 4.4-2: Capacity and Interaction

⇨ Template 4.4-1: Investigating Effective Practices

⇨ Copies of completed Investigation of Effective Practices Planning Form (from Activity 4.3) for each focus area

⇨ Overhead and/or handouts with focus areas, goals, and identified needs (facilitator creates)

⇨ Overhead projector, chart paper, overhead pens or markers

Time Required

Approximately 1 hour

Directions for Facilitators

✱ **Before the Activity:**

— Given the number of focus areas being discussed, decide on the most advantageous grouping of participants for this activity (e.g., by department, by grade level, random groups, full staff).

— Make an overhead and/or a handout listing each focus area, its achievement goals, and its identified needs.

— Use Template 4.4-1 (Investigating Effective Practices) to make one form for each focus area, minimally. (Depending on how you have grouped people, you may need more copies: each brainstorming group could work on a different focus area, all groups could work on the same focus area, or one group could work on all areas.) For each focus area being discussed, start filling out the form, writing in the name of the focus area, the achievement goal, and identified needs. In addition, list any state- or district-required practices or programs that must be included in the plan and place them in the appropriate place on the Venn diagram. *If* there are school-selected materials, practices, professional development, etc. that the school will continue using and that should, therefore, be included in the plan, put these on the Venn diagram as well. (It's important to identify such mandated or continuing practices as soon as possible so that as staff start generating their own ideas of what effective practices to investigate, they can consider how various practices might mesh.) Make an overhead and a poster of the partially completed form for each focus area, as well as enough copies to hand out to work groups.

✱ (5 minutes) Using the completed Investigating Effective Practices Planning Form (Handout 4.3-1 from Activity 4.3), review the staff's involvement in the investigation process. Talk about the task force for each focus area, the steps in the investigation process, the participants' role, and the timeline. Explain that at the close of today's activity a list of potential practices or programs will

106

be given to the group that will be carrying out the actual investigation. State that the proposed effective practices will address the identified needs and will also align with the elements of the Cohen and Ball framework.

✱ (10 minutes) Begin by reviewing the three elements of Cohen and Ball's instructional unit, how they interconnect, and their relationship to student learning. Using Overhead 4.4-1 (Instructional Capacity), review the following points:

— Definition: **Teachers** — When talking about teachers, Cohen and Ball emphasize both their intellectual and interpersonal interactions with students. These include teachers' understanding of knowledge, understanding of the content area, awareness of students' knowledge level and ability to relate to the content, repertoire of teaching strategies, and ability to establish the classroom environment.

— Definition: **Students** — When talking about students, Cohen and Ball emphasize that the resources students bring to the classroom influence what teachers can accomplish. These include students' experience, prior knowledge, habits of mind that influence what they attend to, how they interpret things, and their response to both materials and teachers.

— Definition: **Materials** — Cohen and Ball defined materials broadly as that with which students engage, including texts, problems, tasks, and questions.

— Using Overhead 4.4-2 (Capacity and Interaction), remind participants that interventions are likely to be more effective if they target multiple interactions among the elements of instruction, rather than focusing on one element in isolation.

— Interventions need not act directly on all elements (i.e., teachers, students, and materials. Those that work indirectly on all three elements could be more effective than interventions that work directly only on one element.

✱ (5 minutes) Display the overhead prepared in advance that lists all the focus areas with their student achievement goals and identified needs. Review with the staff the process used for determining identified needs. Explain that the current task is to identify effective practices (e.g., strategies, practices, programs, materials, professional development, general reorganization of resources) that would address the identified needs and that, ideally, would engage more than one element of the instructional unit, thereby increasing the potential effect of the practice on student learning. For example, a suggestion to purchase materials should also incorporate professional development for teachers on how to use the materials.

✱ (10 minutes) Display one of the overheads of a partially completed Investigating Effective Practices form for a focus area. Remind participants that, according to Cohen's and Ball's research, practices affecting more than one element of the instructional unit are more likely to increase student achievement. If there are state- or district-mandated practices already listed on the Venn diagram and/or school-selected practices that will be continued, be sure to explain this to the participants. Give participants a few minutes in their table groups to come up with an effective practice to add to this overhead. Ask each table group to recommend and explain where the practice should be placed on the Venn diagram.

✱ (20 minutes) Tell participants that they will now start filling out a Venn diagram for their assigned focus area, identifying potential practices to address the identified needs and achievement goals in their focus area. Pass out the focus area posters to the appropriate groups, along with enough

107

copies of the partially completed Investigating Effective Practices form for each focus area group. Have each group select a recorder. Give the groups up to 20 minutes to generate ideas for their focus area. The recorder can fill them in on the poster while team members take notes on their Investigating Effective Practices forms. Circulate around the room, questioning participants to ensure that their suggestions are justified and that they are placed in the correct area on the Venn diagram.

✱ (10 minutes) **Closure:** Ask each team to share its focus area, an identified need in that area, a suggested practice, and where it fits on the Venn diagram and why. Review the next steps for further investigation of the proposed strategies and practices. Remind participants that the leadership team or some other smaller group will compile all of the suggestions into a single list, organized by focus area, which will be shared with the full staff before the investigation starts.

Note: Prior to beginning the investigation of effective practices, the leadership team, focus area task force leaders, or some other small group must compile all the ideas from the Venn diagrams into a single list, by focus area, of potential effective practices that will be investigated. This list will later be shared with the full staff. The potential practices could be listed, by focus area, on the overhead created before this activity, which lists all the focus areas, with their respective goals and identified needs. However you list them consider organizing them, by focus area, as follows:

✱ practices to be investigated, including continuing or required practices, which should be identified as such, and

✱ practices that have been suggested but that will not be investigated because they conflict with requirements, are not state-adopted, etc. (be sure to note why a practice will not be investigated).

Distinguish between the required or continuing practices and the suggested practices on the list. Also, be sure to explain why it might have been necessary for some suggested practices to be eliminated even before the investigation (e.g., not a state-adopted program, conflicts with existing professional development, etc.).

INVESTIGATING EFFECTIVE PRACTICES

Purpose and Objectives

There are many steps to conducting an in-depth investigation of proposed effective practices. Sufficient information must be collected to give school staff a sound basis for selecting the practices that will go into the school plan. In this activity, the leadership team or focus area task forces will

* gather and record specific information about all of the suggested practices,

* do an initial rating of the practices to narrow them to a few that will be investigated more deeply,

* conduct a deeper investigation of these practices, and

* make recommendations to the staff about which practices are most likely to successfully address the identified needs of the school community.

Background for Facilitators

Rationale

This activity is designed to help a leadership team or focus area task forces investigate effective practices and make adoption recommendations to the full staff based on substantial factual information. When recommendations are based on concrete, objective information rather than on opinion, there is increased probability that the recommended practices will help the school to realize its goals. And when the rationale for the recommendations is presented to the whole staff, there is greater likelihood of broad ownership and, therefore, more committed implementation.

Activity 4.3 previews the steps in the investigative process and helps teams plan the investigation. That activity must be completed prior to engaging in this one so that the investigation timeline and participants will already be established. The school should also have completed Activity 4.4 wherein participants generate a list of proposed effective practices for addressing identified needs in each focus area and moving the school toward its student achievement goals. This activity — 4.5 — gives step-by-step instructions for completing the investigation. These steps move each focus area investigation team from the comprehensive list of possible practices generated in Activity 4.4 through a specific method for gathering information about each one and narrowing the choices to a few effective practices that will be recommended to the whole staff. The completed investigation forms from this activity are then used in Activity 4.6 for final decision-making.

Source

This activity was developed by WestEd facilitators.

Uses

In this activity, several investigations into effective practices will be going on simultaneously, one for each focus area (e.g., language arts, special education, mathematics). Because the full staff will participate in the final selection of practices to include in the school plan (see Activity 4.6), at some schools it

109

may suffice to have the leadership team carry out this activity. If, on the other hand, building broader ownership of school change is a challenge for your school, you may want to involve a broader array of participants, in which case it makes sense to have task forces carry out the investigations in their respective focus areas. All staff can be associated with one or another of the task forces, but may have varying degrees of involvement (e.g., collector of information, reviewer of information, advisor) depending on time and interest. It will be up to the school to decide who will be involved. If Activity 4.3 was completed, this decision would have been made as the investigation was planned.

Whether members of a leadership team or focus area task forces, *all* participants in this activity stay together for Step 1, wherein a single facilitator sets the stage for the investigations. Subsequent steps, which include the initial research into practices, the rating of practices, and a deeper investigation into a narrowed number of practices, are carried out by small groups (either subsets of the leadership team or individual task forces), each responsible for a different focus area. As these "focus area investigation teams" move forward simultaneously with their investigations, each will need its own facilitator (e.g., the task force leader), and each facilitator will need to have his or her own copies of the relevant overheads and handouts.

Three of the steps in this activity are likely to take place at the school (or wherever most other activities have been conducted). The two steps devoted to researching the practices take place wherever the investigation teams deem necessary (e.g., at the library, in the field, at a home computer, at another school that is using a practice being investigated).

Materials

⇨ Handout 4.5-1: Instructions for Investigating Effective Practices (2 pages)

⇨ Handout 4.5-2: Websites for Investigating Effective School Practices

⇨ Resource 4.5-1: Determining a Rating System for Effective Practices

⇨ Template 4.5-1: Investigation Recording Form

⇨ Overhead (created by facilitator) listing the focus areas and the proposed effective practices to be investigated

⇨ Completed Investigating Effective Practices Planning Form (from Activity 4.3)

⇨ Overhead and handouts (created by facilitator) of Rating System for Effective Practices

⇨ Overhead projector, chart paper, overhead pens or markers

Time Required

This investigation process has a number of steps and must be completed over a period of days. The school's completed Investigating Effective Practices Planning Form (from Activity 4.3) should specify the time available and any deadlines. Each focus area investigation team should review this form before beginning its investigation.

Directions for Facilitators

✱ **Before the Activity:**

— The leadership team or a group representing the focus area task forces must obtain or develop a rating system to use after preliminary research into effective practices to rank the practices and identify a smaller number that warrant more in-depth investigation. If the school or district has a rating system, have the team or group review it to ensure its appropriateness for the current task. If one must be developed, guidelines and a suggested rating system are provided in Resource 4.5-1 (Determining a Rating System for Effective Practices), available on the CD along with overheads and handouts.

— Once the rating system has been chosen, make copies of the instructions for all participants, as well as an overhead.

— Create an overhead based on the outcome of Activity 4.4, listing each focus area and the related effective practices that will be investigated.

— Create an overhead of the completed Investigating Effective Practices Planning Form (from Activity 4.3) and highlight the specific tasks associated with the actual investigation.

— Use Template 4.5-1 (Investigation Recording Form) to make a handout for each practice being considered, writing in the focus area, the effective practice being investigated, and the identified need it is intended to address.

Step 1: Setting the Stage for Investigation (Approximately 1 hour, 20 minutes)

* (15 minutes) Review the role of the focus area investigation teams. Showing the overhead listing the focus areas and proposed effective practices for each one, explain that each team will be investigating the comprehensive list of effective practices for its respective focus area that was generated by the full staff in Activity 4.4. After investigating the listed practices, they will develop a shorter list of recommended practices, which will subsequently be considered by the full staff. Identify any practices that are mandated by the district or state and any school-selected practices that must be continued. Explain that these, too, will be investigated so team members can be sure that additional practices recommended for the plan will be a good fit with required or existing practices. Display the overhead of the completed Investigating Effective Practices Planning Form from Activity 4.3 and review where you are in the overall process of determining effective practices, what steps participants will work through, and the timeline.

* (45 minutes) Using the overhead listing each focus area and the related effective practices that will be investigated, assign the potential practices for investigation to the appropriate focus area investigation teams. It is recommended that team members split into pairs, each investigating a practice. Distribute Handout 4.5-1 (Instructions for Investigating Effective Practices) and copies of the partially completed Investigation Recording Forms to the appropriate pairs. As a group, review each step in the instructions and talk about what information the pairs will collect. Discuss and come to a shared understanding of the task.

* (10 minutes) Discuss with the team members where to find information. Distribute Handout 4.5-2 (Websites for Investigating Effective School Practices). Have team members suggest other sources from which they might obtain additional information.

* (10 minutes) Review the timeline for completion, using the overhead of the Investigating Effective Practices Planning Form, and ask if there are additional questions about the initial review. Remind participants that when this initial information gathering is completed, they will be ranking the practices to select several for in-depth investigation. Ask them to come to the next meeting (see Step 3) with enough copies of each completed Investigation Recording Form for everyone on their investigation team.

Step 2: Find Initial Information About the Effective Practices

Each investigation pair collects information according to the directions on Handout 4.5-1 (Instructions for Investigating Effective Practices) and records the information in the appropriate place on its Investigation Recording Form. Information can be gathered from a variety of sources: personal knowledge, articles, websites (see Handout 4.5-2 [Websites for Investigating Effective School Practices]), and local experts at the school, district, or county office. The pairs should complete this initial investigation by the deadline on the school's Investigating Effective Practices Planning Form. Note: Send a reminder to the task force members about the next meeting and also reminding each investigating pair to bring copies of its recording form for everyone on the investigation team.

Step 3: Rate the Effective Practices and Select Those for Further Investigation (1.75-3 hours depending on the number of practices)

* (15 minutes) Using the overhead developed for Step 1 that lists the focus areas and proposed effective practices for each, review the task participants have just completed. Explain that the next step will be to rank the practices they have investigated with the intent of identifying just a few of the most interesting to investigate more deeply. Let them know the number of practices that the leadership team thought could be investigated more deeply (if addressed in Activity 4.3) or, alternatively, explain what resources (e.g., time) are available to support further investigation. Tell participants that based on the further investigation some potential effective practices might be ruled out or that all the investigated practices might be sent to the full staff as recommended practices to address the identified needs.

* (20-40 minutes, depending on the number of investigations) Ask the investigating pairs to pass out the copies of their completed Investigation Recording Forms. Have the pairs briefly describe their investigations and results. Have them share any surprises or anything unusual they found in their investigations.

* (40-60 minutes, depending on the number of investigations) Pass out the handouts with instructions for rating the effective practices, as determined before the activity. Using the corresponding overhead, explain the rating system. Have investigation team members, again working in pairs, rate all of the practices except those that are mandated. (**Note:** If the task force is smaller than six people, the rating can be done as a group rather than first in pairs and then as a group.) When everyone has finished, have each pair share its ratings and use the overhead that lists the focus areas with proposed effective practices to record the ratings for each practice. If the ratings vary, ask pairs to explain their thinking and ask the team to try to reach consensus about the rating. Continue the discussion until all practices have an agreed-upon rating. Based on the ratings, select which practices will move on to be further investigated. The precise number will be based on the number previously determined by the leadership team or by the resources available for the in-depth investigation.

* (30 minutes) As a group, determine what the in-depth investigation of these selected practices will look like. Explain, for example, that more information about specific steps in implementing a practice could be gathered by visiting or participating in a conference call with the principal and teachers at schools that are using the practice in question. If the practice is some form of professional development, further investigation might entail reviewing a draft agenda or examining participant materials from the organization delivering the professional development. Whatever other research takes place, it's also important to check whether a proposed practice aligns with the school philosophy and existing programs. Finally, the investigation should include a

detailed resource analysis to understand the level of time, personnel, and funding required for implementation of a given practice.

On the overhead, on chart paper, or on blank copies of Handout 4.3-1 (Investigating Effective Practices Planning Form) from Activity 4.3, record what additional steps will be taken and by whom. It may be beneficial here, too, to have teams break into pairs, with each one investigating a particular practice. Tell participants the date of the next meeting, at which they will review the results of the investigation. Remind them that they will be documenting the new information for each practice on their existing Investigation Recording and that at the next meeting they will need to bring enough copies to share with the full team.

> Note: Once plans for additional investigation have been completed and before the next phase of investigation begins, the facilitators for the focus area investigation teams should compare notes to see if there is overlap in planned investigations. For example, if two teams intend to have someone visit another school, the facilitators should get them together to plan a joint visit so as not to overburden the other school or to create unnecessary work for your own staff.

Step 4: Investigate Further

Here the pairs from each focus area investigation team conduct the in-depth investigation into their assigned practice (from Step 3) and log the additional information on the Investigation Recording Form for that practice.

Step 5: Make Final Recommendations (Approximately 1 hour — possibly more, depending on the ability of the team to agree on recommended practices)

* (30 minutes) Explain to team members that the purpose of the meeting is to decide, based on their investigations, which effective practices to recommend to the full staff for inclusion in the school plan (in addition to any required practices). Explain that they could forward all of the practices that have been further investigated or could again use the rating system to rank this smaller group of practices. Tell them that the key is to make sure they recommend only those practices that they believe will effectively address the identified needs in their respective focus area. Ask investigating pairs to pass out copies of their completed Investigation Recording Forms. Have them briefly describe the results of their in-depth investigation, highlighting any new information.

* (30-50 minutes, depending on agreement on recommended practices) Using an overhead or chart paper with all of the *further-investigated practices* listed, lead a discussion of which ones should be forwarded as recommended practices to the full staff. If the investigation team is in agreement, the activity is completed. Go to the Closure.

    If after discussion the investigation team members cannot agree on which practices to recommend, use the Rating System for Effective Practices from Step 3 to rank the practices they researched in depth to see which ones should be forwarded to the full staff for final review. Follow a process similar to that in Step 3.

* (3 minutes) **Closure:** Tell participants the date of the staff meeting at which the recommendations will be shared. Determine who will share the results of the investigation and the basis for their

113

recommendations. Thank participants for their time and the thorough job they have done investigating the practices. Assure them that because of the depth of their investigation the school's plan will be more likely to have an impact on student achievement.

Note: Prior to the meeting at which the full staff will receive recommendations of effective practices from focus area investigation teams, the leadership team, the task force leaders, or some other small group will need to review all of the recommended practices for overlap and/or redundancy and adjust the lists accordingly.

SELECTING EFFECTIVE PRACTICES

Purpose and Objectives

In this activity, staff will make final decisions about a cluster of effective practices in each focus area that they think will help them reach their student achievement goals and should, therefore, be included in the school plan. Members of focus area investigation teams have been collecting information on proposed practices and have narrowed the options to a handful. Information gathered during the investigation phase will be shared and discussed during this activity, and each proposed effective practice will be rated according to specific criteria. Based upon that rating, a final decision will be made about which practices in each focus area to include in the school plan. In this activity, participants will

* share and discuss information gathered during the investigation phase on each recommended practice for each focus area, and

* make a final decision on a cluster of effective practices to include in the plan for each focus area.

Background for Facilitators

Rationale

Making the final decision about which effective practices to include in the school plan is the culmination of the investigation phase of the school planning process. In this activity the recommendations of separate focus area investigation teams are presented to the whole staff. While the full staff brainstormed lists of potential practices to be considered for the plan (see Activity 4.4), they have not yet seen the results of the investigations into these practices. Here, the investigation teams present their recommendations for a set of practices they believe will effectively address the identified needs and, thus, help the school reach its student achievement goals in their respective focus areas. Staff review these, make the final selection, and, in the process, renew their commitment to the school's goals.

Because ownership leads to a deeper level of implementation and support, the critical issue in this activity is how to build ownership if time is short or if there is little choice involved in the recommended practices, either because of the number of state or district mandates or because investigation has identified only a few viable options.

Source

This activity was developed by WestEd facilitators.

References

Cohen, D. K., & Ball, D. L. (1999). *Instruction, capacity, and improvement* (Consortium for Policy Research in Education Research Report Series, #RR-043). Philadelphia: Consortium for Policy Research in Education. Available at http://www.cpre.org/Publications/rr43.pdf. Last accessed on June 9, 2006.

115

Uses

Activity 4.6 entails a detailed process that must be completed for each focus area. Depending on the size of your staff and the number of focus areas being addressed, you may need to have more than one focus area meeting underway at the same time, in which case you may need to draw on focus area leaders to facilitate.

Because it is essential that each investigated practice within a focus area be carefully considered for inclusion in the final plan, make sure there is adequate time to do so — even if it requires extending the decision-making process for a given focus area into a second session. It is also important to consider who should be involved in making the decision for each focus area. Although the full staff will be involved in the overall activity, it is not necessary to have all staff involved in all decisions. It may be more appropriate to have smaller subgroups making decisions about the practices in their respective focus areas. For example, in secondary schools that use departmentalization, it may not be appropriate to have the English department participate in a decision about math. However, there would still need to be conversation between the two departments at some point, to examine how the identified practices in their respective focus areas interrelate and, together, move the school toward its goals.

Materials

- ⇨ Overhead 4.6-1: Steps in the Decision-Making Process
- ⇨ Overhead 4.6-2: Instructional Capacity
- ⇨ Overhead 4.6-3: Capacity and Interaction
- ⇨ Overhead 4.6-4: Focus on Teachers
- ⇨ Overhead 4.6-5: Focus on Students
- ⇨ Overhead 4.6-6: Focus on Materials
- ⇨ Template 4.6-1: Proposed Plan Outline
- ⇨ Overhead of completed Investigating Effective Practices Planning Form (from Activity 4.3)
- ⇨ Overheads of the completed Investigation Recording Forms (Template 4.5-1) from Activity 4.5, with paper copies for participants
- ⇨ Any written literature gathered in the investigation
- ⇨ Proposed Plan Outline on chart paper (one for each group)
- ⇨ Overhead projector, chart paper, overhead pens or markers, colored stickers

Time Required

The number and length of sessions will vary, depending on the number of focus areas and the number of decisions to be made in each one. A session for one focus area will take approximately 3 hours.

Directions for Facilitators

✱ **Before the Activity:**

- — The activity is organized into six steps, from setting the stage and reviewing the investigation results to selecting a cluster of related effective practices to meet the identified needs in each focus area. There are several variations to the process depending on how easily staff agree about which practices to include in the school plan. Review the instructions very carefully in advance so you can choose which variation to use and, thereby, ensure a smooth decision-making process that creates cross-staff ownership for the effective practices ultimately included in the school plan.

— Determine who will be involved in the review of recommended practices for each focus area. Base the decision on several factors: available time, the relevancy of the focus area to particular staff (e.g., practices related to English learners may be relevant to a broader number of staff than are practices related to math), and the breadth of ownership needed for successful implementation. Set up meetings accordingly.

— Because it is important to have in-depth discussion of the practices, the activity is written as if you will divide participants into a number of small working groups, each discussing the same practices. If relatively few people are participating in total (i.e., 9 or less), adjust the steps accordingly, using strategies appropriate for a single group to achieve consensus on the final cluster of effective practices. If there is only one group the activity will also require less time because, for example, there will be no need for small groups to share their decisions with the whole group.

— For each focus area to be discussed, create a chart with the headings from Template 4.6-1 (Proposed Plan Outline). Prepare each chart by listing the focus area, related student achievement goals, and identified needs. (If more than one group is working on the same focus area, make a chart for each one.)

— Collect the completed Investigation Recording Forms (from Activity 4.5) and sort them by focus area. Make an overhead of each one with sufficient paper copies for members of the group discussing that focus area.

— Make an overhead of the completed Investigating Effective Practices Planning Form from Activity 4.3.

Step 1: Setting the Stage for Decision-Making (20 minutes — whole group)

✱ (10 minutes) Using an overhead of the completed Investigating Effective Practices Planning Form from Activity 4.3, briefly remind participants of the steps that have been taken to identify and research the recommended practices they will be discussing. If pertinent, tell participants about the other groups that are meeting and the focus areas they are discussing.

✱ (10 minutes) Using Overhead 4.6-1 (Steps in the Decision-Making Process), describe the process that they will use to determine clusters of effective practices that address the identified needs and that will help the school reach agreed-upon student achievement goals. Emphasize how the process is aimed at developing shared ownership for the decisions and creating a systemic response to the identified needs.

Step 2: Reviewing the Investigation Findings (Approximately 80 minutes, depending on the number of recommended practices that are shared — whole group and, if you have assigned them, small groups)

✱ (Approximately 30 minutes — whole group) Give each participant a copy of the completed Investigation Recording Form (from Activity 4.5) for the focus area to be discussed during this session. Have overheads available as well. Have a lead person from the focus area investigation team review the information for each recommended effective practice. If the team conducted site

117

visits or spoke with schools implementing the practice, this should be shared, too. Make sure it is noted if a practice being discussed is required by the district or state.

✳ (10 minutes — whole group) Encourage staff to ask clarifying questions. Explain that this is not the time to express opinions, only to gather more information.

✳ (15-20 minutes — small groups) Allow time for the groups to discuss the effective practices with the intent of developing a clear understanding of each practice and what would be required to implement it. Have them write any probing questions on chart paper. These questions should help participants to think deeply about the individual practices and about how one practice compares and/or relates to another. This is not the time to express opinions, but to critically examine the practices in comparison to each other.

✳ (20 minutes — whole group) Have each small group present its questions. Investigation team members and other staff who helped investigate the practices answer questions. Invite other staff members with factual information to share what they know.

> **Note: If there are questions that cannot be answered and it is important to know the answer prior to making a decision, the meeting should be adjourned and the group should reconvene after the answer is found.**

Step 3: Understanding Clustering Practices (20 minutes — whole group)

✳ (20 minutes) Point out that when practices are used together in a related cluster to address multiple facets of a problem, they are likely to be most effective in addressing identified needs.

— Draw participants' attention to the section on the Investigation Recording Form (from Activity 4.5) labeled *Implications of Implementation*. Specifically, point out what is listed as necessary to fully implement the effective practice. Show Overhead 4.6-2 (Instructional Capacity) and remind staff about the Cohen and Ball article and how the interaction of materials, students, and teachers yields greater impact on student learning than does any one of those factors individually.

— Next, display Overhead 4.6-3 (Capacity and Interaction). Give staff a few minutes to read it.

— Display Overhead 4.6-4 (Focus on Teachers). Point out the last sentence: *Consequently, teachers' opportunities to develop and extend their knowledge and capabilities can considerably affect instruction by affecting how well teachers make use of students and materials.* Draw participants' attention to the Implications of Implementation for one of the focus areas where professional development is listed as a necessary support. Ask them to explain how this relates to the highlighted sentence. (The point here is to talk about the importance of professional development related both to the materials they use and to effective strategies for the students they serve.)

— Display Overhead 4.6-5 (Focus on Students) and point out the following sentence: *Students bring experience, prior knowledge, and habits of mind, and these influence how they apprehend, interpret, and respond to materials and teachers.* Draw participants' attention to the Implications of Implementation for one of the focus areas where tapping students' interest — drawing on their experience or eliciting their perceptions — is listed as a necessary support for effective implementation of the recommended practice. Ask them to explain how this relates to the highlighted sentence. (The point here is to talk about how student self-perception, motivation, and interest can be leveraged to more effectively implement the recommended practices and improve student achievement.)

— Display Overhead 4.6-6 (Focus on Materials) and point out the following sentence: *… students' and teachers' interactions with this material comprise the enacted — which is to say, the actual or effective — curriculum. These material technologies influence instructional capacity by constraining or enabling students' and teachers' opportunities to learn and teach.* Draw participants' attention to the Implication of Implementation for one of the focus areas where there are scheduling changes, the use of instructional grouping, or a change in structure that affects the way teachers and students interact with the curriculum. Ask them to explain how this relates to the highlighted sentence. (The point here is to talk about changing how teachers and students interact around the curriculum. This could include issues of access to curriculum for all students.)

Step 4: Composing Clusters of Effective Practices (50 minutes — whole group and small group)

✱ (15 minutes — whole group) Remind participants that the task for today is to select a cluster of effective practices that will best address the identified needs and, therefore, improve student achievement in the focus area. Using Template 4.6-1 (Proposed Plan Outline), explain to participants that their job in the small groups is to create both a first and a second choice cluster of practices (which may have overlapping elements) to address the identified need(s). Tell them the whole group will ultimately need to reach consensus on one cluster of effective practices for each focus area and having a first and second choice may make the decision-making process easier. Tell them that they must carefully study the information about the effective practices that is documented on the completed Investigation Recording Forms from Activity 4.5 and decide which ones will best meet their students' needs. In doing so, they must look for alignment between practices and must also select support activities that will help ensure successful implementation of the practices. You might explain the process this way:

> *For example, maybe one effective practice listed is the use of project-based learning, shown to improve students' motivation in math as well as their math skills. Your group may decide to cluster this effective practice with the selection of a new textbook that can be used with project-based learning and the accompanying professional development for teachers. This approach would draw on multiple areas in Cohen and Ball's model including increased student motivation and how teachers and students interact with instructional materials.*

Suggestions for implementation support activities for a practice may be found in the focus area task force recommendations for accompanying activities as listed in the Implications of Implementation portion of the Investigation Recording Form (from Activity 4.5). They may also come out of participants' own analysis of the list of effective practices as influenced by the Cohen and Ball framework from Overhead 4.6-2 (Instructional Capacity).

✱ (35 minutes — small groups) Give each group a copy of the chart created in advance from Template 4.6-1 (Proposed Plan Outline) for this focus area. Tell them they will write on this chart their first and second choice cluster of effective practices. Ask for questions before they begin. Allow 30 minutes for this portion of the activity. Monitor the groups' work, making sure they clearly label their first and second choice clusters and use all of the available resources: the Investigation Recording Forms, the task force members in their groups, the Cohen and Ball filters, and any additional information generated in Steps 2 and 3.

Step 5: Determining Clusters of Effective Practices (Time varies greatly depending on the degree of agreement among staff — whole group activity)

✱ (20 minutes — whole group) Display each group's chart of proposed clusters of effective practices. Allow time for participants to walk around and review each one. During this time, also review the charts yourself to determine next steps based on the degree of agreement or disagreement evidenced in the charts.

As groups review and process the suggested plans, an "aha!" moment may occur with staff gravitating to one particular plan. In this instance, you may hear comments like: "That's a really good idea," "I never thought of combining things in that way," or "Wow, that really gets at all aspects of the problem!" If this occurs, note which plan outline is attracting the attention and use this information in the decision-making process. Or you may see common threads across the charts. Note any common elements to use in the next section of the activity.

Note: The next step in determining what cluster of effective practices to include in the school plan depends in part on the consistency or, conversely, variety of proposed clusters and in part on how participants appear to respond to the proposed clusters during the gallery walk.

5a. If all groups have identified the same cluster of effective practices as either their first or second choice or if participants are gravitating to a single plan:

Display the chart of the plan that participants appear to be favoring. Describe what you heard or observed during the review. Lead a brief discussion about the attractions of this cluster of activities. Use a "Fist to Five" to check how each individual feels about this plan. If the decision is clear and unanimous, move to Step 6a, Closure.

5b. If across the groups there are two to three different clusters of practices recommended or participants appear to be split two or three ways in their review of the plans:

Explain that because no single cluster appears to stand out for participants, they will participate in an individual forced-choice activity to decide which cluster to include in the plan.

Post the charts displaying what appear to be the two most popular clusters based on what you observed during the review. Explain to participants why you selected these particular clusters. Ask the authoring groups to explain their thinking in creating these clusters. Lead a discussion about advantages, disadvantages, and possible changes for each cluster. Give every participant a sticker and ask them to place their stickers under their preferred effective practice. If there is a clear preference, the decision is made. Proceed to Step 6, Closure.

If there is no clear choice, facilitate further discussion about why the staff is split. Maybe they need more information. Perhaps the activity needs to be repeated for individual practices (rather than clusters). Whatever the case, getting to the heart of the matter is important so a decision can be made that staff feel good about. Continue the conversation until there is either an agreed-upon cluster, or the group has agreed to a process for making the final decision at a later date. If a cluster has been chosen, go to Step 6a, Closure. If more work is needed before agreeing on a cluster, go to Step 6b, Closure.

5c. If across the groups there are four or five different clusters posted, if participants seem similarly split in their review of the clusters, and/or if there is no consistency across proposed clusters other than a few common practices:

Have each group stand in front of its own chart and explain the thinking behind the clustering. Allow other participants to ask clarifying questions. Point out commonalities and correct any misunderstandings. After all groups are done, reconvene the individual small groups. Ask them to consider what they have just learned and then create a cluster that addresses the issues they heard during the process.

Have each group display its new recommended cluster. If there is consensus, the decision is made and you can move to Step 6, Closure. If two or three choices emerge, use the forced-choice activity described in 5b. If there is still wide disparity, there may be other issues at play, such as lack of clear information, personal agendas, or distrust across the faculty. Ask if any clarification is needed about the final recommendations. Answer questions as they come up. Next, recommend that there be an anonymous, individual voting process. Go to Step 6c, Closure.

5d. If there are more than five clusters of recommended practices and no apparent agreement among participants:

Use the process in 5c, looking carefully for any underlying issues that may be influencing staff thinking. If the roadblock seems to be lack of understanding, try the process for clarification and reconceptualization of clusters outlined in 5c. If agreement is reached, go to Step 6a. If not, go to Step 6b or 6c depending on the outcome.

If the roadblock appears, instead, to be personal agendas or distrust, recommend that there be an anonymous, individual voting process on two clusters that the full group generates together. Depending on the time available, you might facilitate the development of two new clusters now. If not, tell participants they will develop the new clusters at a follow-up meeting and you will let them know the date and time.

Step 6: Closure (10 minutes — whole group)

6a. (10 minutes) If a cluster of effective practices has been selected, tell participants that the next step is to determine the specific details for implementation, including the allocation of resources, the timeline, and the persons who will be involved in the implementation. A group will write these details in the form of an action plan. Ask for volunteers to carry out this portion of the work. Assure participants that they will be informed of all decisions and will continue to be involved in the remainder of the process.

6b. (10 minutes) If the group has agreed on a process for choosing a cluster at a later date, review the agreed-upon process and, if another meeting is needed, tell participants you will let them know the date.

6c. (10 minutes) If an individual vote is needed, explain how and when this will occur. Review the timeline for the voting, the criteria for selecting the final cluster, and who will be handling each step. Tell them that the recommended clusters will be left on display where they can review them and discuss them during grade-level meetings or at other times. Let them know who was on the task force and invite them to approach any of the task force members with any further questions they may have.

CONSTRUCTING AN EFFECTIVE ACTION PLAN

Purpose and Objectives

Now that the school has identified the various components of its improvement plan, the task is to bring everything together into a coherent program of practices that will address its identified needs and facilitate the improvement process. The plan must also include all necessary implementation information (e.g., who is responsible, timeline). Some districts or states have a required format for schools' action plan. For those that don't, this activity helps participants reflect on the most appropriate format to support their change effort.

There is no "best" layout for an action plan. Depending on the nature and needs of different schools and depending on any state or local requirements by which they must abide, the way in which their action plans are laid out will differ. The primary purpose of the action plan is to be a useful tool for guiding school staff in implementing agreed-upon effective practices and support activities. Having a clear and comprehensive action plan helps ensure the effectiveness and efficiency of a school's improvement efforts.

In this activity, participants

* become familiar with different templates for recording an action plan,

* learn how to create a complete script for their school's improvement efforts, and

* create a template specific to their school.

123

Background for Facilitators

Rationale

Developing and implementing a school improvement plan is an iterative process; if a plan is to be effective, improvement efforts must be ongoing and continuous, their effect reviewed and documented in the course of implementation. Having all improvement-related information in one complete document provides a clear picture of the entire improvement endeavor, its goals, and how all practices and support activities are intended to fit together in moving the school toward those goals. This helps prevent fragmentation of effort and, over time, makes it easier to identify areas of weakness or inconsistency. Having one comprehensive document also makes updating information and keeping track of implementation activities much easier. Using an electronic template can be especially helpful for easily updating the plan.

Sources

This activity was developed by WestEd facilitators.

Uses

This activity is intended for whomever will be writing up the action plan, whether the principal, members of the leadership or data team, or some combination. If the district or state requires that a particular format be used, a school need not do this activity unless they want to contrast the samples provided with required format and have a discussion about the relative merits of each.

Activity Directions

Materials

⇨ Overhead 4.7-1: Key Points: A Clear and Comprehensive Action Plan

⇨ Handout 4.7-1: Constructing an Effective Action Plan (2 pages)

⇨ Handout 4.7-2: Action Plan Template, Example #1

⇨ Handout 4.7-3: Action Plan Template, Example #2 (2 pages)

Time Required

Approximately 1 hour, depending on length of discussion

Directions for Facilitators

✴ (10 minutes) Using Overhead 4.7-1 (Key Points: A Clear and Comprehensive Action Plan), review the key points for why a coherent and comprehensive action plan is important to successful implementation and improved student achievement.

✴ (20 minutes) Pass out Handout 4.7-1 (Constructing an Effective Action Plan) and Handouts 4.7-2 and 4.7-3, the two Template Examples.

Ask participants to take 15 minutes to review the two Template Examples. Explain that they should contrast the two templates by looking at what information is included, how that information is organized, and the order in which the information appears. Ask participants to consider which format would be most helpful to them if they were new to the school and were charged with implementing the action plan. Remind participants that they don't have to choose one or the other but could, instead, create a modified template with elements from each example or something completely different. Tell them to take notes on Handout 4.7-1 (Constructing an Effective Action Plan).

✴ (15 minutes) Facilitate a discussion of the differences, similarities, and the relative merits of each template. Ask participants to discuss different aspects of a template (e.g., organization, type of information included) and identify what they think would be most helpful in implementing an action plan.

✴ (10 minutes) Have participants decide what layout or format they will use for their action plan and implementation steps. Tell participants that they can create their own action plan format that includes elements of each of the samples or, perhaps, something that was not included in either.

✴ (2 minutes) **Closure:** Tell participants that in the next activity they will work on how to write implementation or action steps with sufficient detail to make the steps comprehensible for those who must carry them out.

DEVELOPING CLEAR AND COMPREHENSIVE IMPLEMENTATION STEPS

Purpose and Objectives

Implementation steps are the specific actions a school will take to carry out the agreed-upon effective practices that are intended to address the identified needs in a focus area. In an effective school plan, the implementation steps are the foundation for change and school improvement. Care must be taken in developing them. Otherwise schools risk having implementation steps that are too cumbersome and/or too complicated to follow or that do not contain enough information to drive change. By working through the development of each step in a deliberate manner, schools can ensure that the flow from one step to the next is smooth, efficient, and logical.

As a result of this activity, participants will

* understand different approaches to developing implementation steps,

* realize that different practices may call for different approaches to developing implementation steps, and

* develop a set of guidelines for generating clear and comprehensive implementation steps.

Background for Facilitators

Rationale

Clarity and comprehensiveness are essential characteristics of an improvement plan; anyone must be able to read it, understand it, and know what needs to be done. This is important even for staff who have been involved in the development of a plan, but it is especially so for any new people, whether principal, teachers, or others who come to a school after the plan has been written. Without clear direction about each step that must be taken, successful implementation will be elusive. An effective set of implementation steps addresses the following questions:

* What does the fully implemented practice (e.g., activity, strategy, program) look like? What elements or sub-steps are there?

* Who will be responsible for making sure that each element is fully implemented?

* What people, time, and/or materials will be needed for implementation?

* What is the timeline for implementation?

* How much will it cost?

There is no one perfect approach to developing steps that address these questions. In this activity, participants consider different approaches and develop guidelines for how they will develop their own implementation steps.

Source

This activity was developed by WestEd facilitators.

Uses

This activity should be completed by those writing the action plan. This is generally the principal, members of the leadership or data team, or some combination and should include representatives of each focus area task force. Alternatively, the focus area task forces, if charged with writing the section of the plan related to their focus area, might participate as a group in the activity.

Activity Directions

Materials

⇨ Overhead 4.8-1: Clear and Comprehensive Implementation Steps

⇨ Handout 4.8-1: Developing Clear and Comprehensive Implementation Steps — Example #1

⇨ Overhead 4.8-2: Developing Clear and Comprehensive Implementation Steps — Example #1

⇨ Handout 4.8-2: Developing Clear and Comprehensive Implementation Steps — Example #2

⇨ Overhead 4.8-3: Developing Clear and Comprehensive Implementation Steps — Example #2

⇨ Handout 4.8-3: Developing Clear and Comprehensive Implementation Steps — Example #3

⇨ Overhead 4.8-4: Developing Clear and Comprehensive Implementation Steps — Example #3

⇨ Chart paper or blank overheads, markers

Time Required

1-1.5 hours, depending on length of discussion

Directions for Facilitators

> Note: Although they have the same titles, the handout and the corresponding overhead for each of the three examples of "Developing Clear and Comprehensive Implementation Steps" are not exactly the same.

✱ (15 minutes) Explain the importance of carefully developed implementation steps: Steps must be sufficiently clear and comprehensive to ensure that anyone charged with implementing the plan (whether or not the person helped write the plan) will understand exactly what needs to be done, who is responsible, and what resources should be used. Using Overhead 4.8-1 (Clear and Comprehensive Implementation Steps), describe the important components of good implementation steps.

✱ (15 minutes) Provide each participant with a copy of Handout 4.8-1 (Developing Clear and Comprehensive Implementation Steps — Example #1). Review with participants the directions on the handout. Reiterate why it is so important for implementation steps to be well written, complete, and focused if they are to be useful in guiding school improvement. Tell participants to refer to the guiding questions about implementation steps on Overhead 4.8-1 (Clear and Comprehensive Implementation Steps). Ask them to work with partners to answer the questions on the handout for Example #1. Have them make notes on the handout and, if they want to, revise the implementation step. Tell them that in reading this example they should also be considering what format or types of information they want to be sure to include in their own implementation steps. Tell participants that they will have 10 minutes to work. Monitor conversations. Stop sooner if participants appear to be finishing sooner.

* (15 minutes) Display Overhead 4.8-2 (Developing Clear and Comprehensive Implementation Steps — Example #1) and have participants share their responses to the questions and any additions they might have proposed. Make notes on the overhead. Push participants to show how their additional information or proposed revisions would make the steps clearer or more comprehensive. Also, push participants to identify formats or types of information they want to be sure to include in their own implementation steps. Note these on chart paper.

* (20 minutes) Repeat the process for the second example (Handout 4.8-2 and Overhead 4.8-3 [Developing Clear and Comprehensive Implementation Steps — Example #2]). Allow 10 minutes for partner work and 10 minutes for sharing. Continue to build the list of guidelines for the school's implementation steps.

* (20 minutes) Repeat the process for the third example (Handout 4.8-3 and Overhead 4.8-4 [Developing Clear and Comprehensive Implementation Steps — Example #3]). Emphasize that there must be a sufficient level of detail so that even someone new to the school could understand the plan and be able to implement it. Allow 10 minutes for partner work and 10 minutes for sharing. Complete the list of guidelines for the school's implementation steps.

* (5 minutes) **Closure:** Tell participants that the list of guidelines for developing implementation steps will be typed up and distributed to them to use as they write the steps for their respective focus areas. Remind them that, within these guidelines, there is still flexibility in both format and level of detail used, depending on the complexity or breadth of the practice they're writing about. In closing, mention once more that the aim is to make the implementation plan clear and easy to follow, no matter who is reading it.

127

COMPLETING IMPLEMENTATION STEPS: ALIGNING RESOURCES

Purpose and Objectives

Once practices for the school improvement plan have been identified, school staff will need to allocate resources to each one in order to carry them all out. In a successful school improvement plan, all existing school and district resources — time, money, staff, and even space — should be put on the table for consideration.

It is true that bringing about significant improvement in low-performing schools requires meaningful change, pushing people to do some things, perhaps *many* things, differently. Changing the school's focus may call for significant shifts in the use of resources, and districts and schools may have to reallocate resources that have long been committed to previously perceived priorities. In considering the use of resources to support the school's improvement plan, staff may need to make some difficult decisions. They should not be afraid to think creatively about the resources they have and need in order to meet their goals.

In this activity, participants will

* review available resources,

* align resources with needs,

* identify resource gaps, and

* adjust and align the resources to support the implementation steps.

Background for Facilitators

Rationale

The key to allocating resources for implementing agreed-upon practices is to develop a budget, create schedules, and allot resources *after* implementation steps have been conceptualized. Tailoring the improvement plan to the existing resources will limit what will be accomplished. By identifying the resources needed for implementation of each step and identifying any gaps between what is needed and what the school already has, school leaders can respond accordingly. In the case of identified resource gaps, they may need to exercise some creativity in locating additional resources or may need to revisit and reconsider the implementation steps.

Sources

This activity was developed by WestEd facilitators.

References

van Heusden Hale, S. (2000). *Comprehensive school reform: Research-based strategies to achieve high standards.* San Francisco: WestEd.

129

Odden, A. (1999). *School finances: Better use of resources*. Sacramento, CA: California Association of School Board Officials. Available at http://www.casbo.org/oddendec99.htm. Last accessed on June 21, 2006.

Uses

The process of allocating, identifying gaps, and aligning resources is best undertaken by the group of people charged with writing the school plan. These people are most often on focus area task forces or make up the leadership team. Resource allocation should not be handled for each focus area separately. Rather, resources for the entire school plan should be considered together and allocated across the focus areas.

It might be wise to do this activity over two sessions. The Overview and Part 1, Review and Allocate Resources, could be done in the first session. If it turns out that resource gaps exist, Part 2, Fill Gaps, could be done at a different time.

Activity Directions

Materials

- ⇨ Overhead 4.9-1: Reallocating Resources
- ⇨ Overhead 4.9-2: Types of Resources
- ⇨ Overhead 4.9-3: Factors for Allocating Resources
- ⇨ Handout 4.9-1: Aligning Resources — Take Stock of Resources
- ⇨ Handout 4.9-2: Aligning Resources — Allocate Resources
- ⇨ Handout 4.9-3: Thinking Outside the Box (2 pages)
- ⇨ Overhead 4.9-4: Thinking Outside the Box
- ⇨ Overhead 4.9-5: Aligning Resources — Allocate Resources
- ⇨ Overhead 4.9-6: If a Gap in Resources Still Remains…
- ⇨ Handout 4.9-4: If a Gap in Resources Still Remains…
- ⇨ Handout 4.9-5: Aligning Resources — Fill Gaps
- ⇨ Chart paper, copies of school budgets, draft school implementation steps

Time

Approximately 3 hours: 20 minutes for the Overview; 1.5 hours for Part 1; 70 minutes for Part 2; 10 minutes for Closure

Directions for Facilitators

✱ Before the Activity:

— Obtain and make copies of the implementation steps for each focus area. If there are more than seven participants, assign participants to small groups of no more than six, with some representation from each focus area task force in each group.

— The principal or some member of the leadership team should fill out Handout 4.9-1 (Aligning Resources — Take Stock of Resources), listing all available resources. Then, in addition to making enough copies of the completed handout for all participants, make a poster-sized chart reflecting the resource categories and information from the completed handout. Leave enough space under each resource category to add any other resources identified in Part 1 of the activity. Post the chart on the wall.

— In Part 1, participants will review the completed version of Handout 4.9-1 (Aligning Resources — Take Stock of Resources) and may well identify additional resources that should be included. They will be asked to add the resources to their own handouts and you will add them to the wall chart. If Part 2 is done immediately thereafter, have participants keep their augmented resource lists to use in Part 2. However, if Part 2 takes place at a later date, you may want to create a new handout with *all* identified resources listed and pass copies out during Part 2.

✱ (20 minutes) **Overview and Key Points:** Using Overhead 4.9-1 (Reallocating Resources), explain the importance of resource allocation to the successful implementation of a school improvement plan. Emphasize the importance of being broad and comprehensive and of thinking outside of the box, especially in thinking about funding sources. Using Overhead 4.9-2 (Types of Resources), remind people of the range of resources. Finally, using Overhead 4.9-3 (Factors for Allocating Resources), review the various considerations that will influence how they allocate resources.

Explain that the group will be doing this activity in two parts: reviewing resources and allocating them to implementation of the plan, and then examining how to fill any resource gaps that become evident.

Part 1: Review and Allocate Resources (1.5–2 hours)

✱ (15 minutes) Distribute copies of the completed version of Handout 4.9-1 (Aligning Resources — Take Stock of Resources). Review the directions on the handout and explain how the list was completed. Ask participants to spend 5 minutes in small groups (or with partners) reviewing and adding to the list. Have each group share its results, highlighting any creative or "unusual" resources. As they are shared, add each additional resource to the wall chart, listing it under the appropriate heading. Ask participants to add the resources to their handouts as well, because they will need the more-complete list of resources as they begin the allocation process.

✱ (15 minutes) Provide copies of Handout 4.9-2 (Aligning Resources — Allocate Resources). Explain the task to participants, using the directions on the handout. Emphasize the importance of having adequate resources to implement the plan, and encourage creative and atypical allocation strategies. Give participants Handout 4.9-3 (Thinking Outside the Box). Using corresponding Overhead 4.9-4, review the questions. Tell participants to keep these in mind as they allocate resources.

✱ (30 minutes) Have participants complete Handout 4.9-2 (Aligning Resources — Allocate Resources), either in their small groups or, if there are fewer than eight participants, as a whole group. There may be several iterations so have extra copies of this handout available.

✱ (30 minutes) If participants have worked in small groups, have them share their results and creative solutions or allocations. Record the results on Overhead 4.9-5 (Aligning Resources — Allocate Resources).

131

✱ (15 minutes) If all the resource needs for the implementation steps appear to be met, tell participants that they can now add these budget components to the appropriate section of the school improvement plan. Skip Part 2 and move to Closure. If there are implementation steps still in need of resources and none are available, highlight these implementation steps on the overhead. Explain that participants will need to complete Part 2 of this activity, in which they will consider how to cover these resources gaps.

Part 2: Fill Gaps (70 minutes)

✱ (10 minutes) If Part 2 is being done at a later date, remind participants that previous work on resource allocation revealed resource gaps. Review the gaps that were identified at the end of Part 1. Remind participants that it is important to develop strategies for filling the gaps. Review the questions and other notes on Overhead 4.9-6 (If a Gap in Resources Still Remains…). Refer participants to corresponding Handout 4.9-4, which has similar questions and additional recommendations.

✱ (30 minutes) Provide copies of Handout 4.9-5 (Aligning Resources — Fill Gaps) and the most complete version of Handout 4.9-2 (Aligning Resources — Allocate Resources) from Part 1. If there are more than seven people, have participants work in small groups. Otherwise, you can lead the conversation. Review the instructions on Handout 4.9-5 (Aligning Resources — Fill Gaps) and have participants complete the handout, making corresponding changes to Handout 4.9-2 (Aligning Resources — Allocate Resources) as well.

✱ (30 minutes) If participants have worked in small groups, have them share their results and strategies. Facilitate the conversation until the gaps are filled and/or decisions have been made about adapting the implementation steps. This may require scheduling additional sessions if, for example, the staff needs to be consulted about a substantial change to an implementation step or additional information needs to be obtained about adapting a practice to fit available resources. When all of the resource needs for the implementation steps are covered, tell participants that they can now add these budget components to their section of the action plan.

✱ (10 minutes) **Closure:** Tell participants to complete their portion of the action plan by adding the budget items. Determine when and how to share the plan with the school community. Consider using Tool 2.2 (Communicating With Constituents) to determine how this will be done.

Module 5: Implement, Monitor, and Evaluate

ACTIVITY 5.1

ARE WE DOING WHAT WE SAID WE WOULD DO? — MONITORING THE ACTION PLAN

Purpose and Objectives

This activity provides participants with a process for monitoring the overall implementation of their school improvement plan (i.e., their action plan). Specifically, participants will

* review the types of data they will need to monitor implementation,

* establish procedures for monitoring implementation, and

* set a schedule for monitoring and reporting information to stakeholders.

Background for Facilitators

Rationale

Too often, plans are written — sometimes multiple plans for one school — and then get safely tucked on a shelf out of sight and out of mind. Continuous improvement depends not just on the creation of an action plan but on thoughtful implementation with ongoing monitoring, review and, as needed, revision. Schools must ask and answer three questions:

1. Are we doing what we said we would do in our action plan?

2. Are we doing it well?

3. Is it making a difference in our student achievement?

This activity, as well as Activities 5.2 and 5.3, provides tools to help leadership and data teams systematically respond to these questions. This activity helps teams determine how they will answer the first question. Activity 5.2 helps schools select a few high-leverage practices from their plan and conduct an in-depth analysis of their implementation. Activity 5.3 offers a process for setting student achievement benchmarks so schools can answer the third question.

This activity assumes that leadership teams have some prior knowledge about types of data, about their school improvement or action plan, and about the school stakeholders. A refresher course on types of data is available in Activity 1.10. Activity 1.12 helps a team figure out what data are available to them and in what format. Tool 3.3b, a classroom observation tool, and Tool 3.3c, a survey, can be used to generate new data.

Note: SchoolForward: An Online System for Maintaining Continuous School Improvement is an implementation and monitoring tool for action plans. Once a school inputs its plan, the tool provides built-in implementation and monitoring support. Because it is web-based, this tool allows users to view a plan in different ways (e.g., by goals, by objectives, by person responsible). It also includes a comprehensive assessment to help schools determine if their plan is ready for implementation. For more information on SchoolForward, go to http://www.schoolforward.org.

Source

This activity was developed by WestEd facilitators.

Uses

In most cases, monitoring the implementation of an improvement or action plan falls to a leadership or data team. The activity is designed to help a team plan its monitoring system.

Activity Directions

Materials

- ⇨ Overhead 5.1-1: After the Planning
- ⇨ Overhead 5.1-2: The Monitoring and Implementation Phase
- ⇨ Overhead 5.1-3: Data Types and Data Sources
- ⇨ Handout 5.1-1: Data Types and Data Sources
- ⇨ Handout 5.1-2: Monitoring Checklist
- ⇨ Overhead 5.1-4: Communicating the Findings
- ⇨ Handout 5.1-3: Communicating the Findings
- ⇨ Copies of the Action Plan for each team member

Time Required

1.5-2 hours, depending on the length of the action plan

Directions for Facilitators

* **Before the Activity:**

    — Make copies of the school improvement or action plan for all participants.

    — Fill out the left-hand column (i.e., Action Plan Implementation Steps) of Handout 5.1-2 (Monitoring Checklist) and make an overhead of the partially completed checklist.

* (10 minutes) In setting the stage, use Overhead 5.1-1 (After the Planning) to underscore the importance of monitoring the implementation of the action plan. Explain that there are multiple

levels of monitoring. Using Overhead 5.1-2 (The Monitoring and Implementation Phase), tell participants that in this activity they will be setting up a system to answer the first question: Are we doing what we said we would do in our action plan?

✴ (5 minutes) Pass out Handout 5.1-1 (Data Types and Data Sources). Using corresponding Overhead 5.1-3, briefly review the four types of data and some of their sources. Tell participants that in determining the degree to which practices from the action plan have been implemented, most of the data sources they will need will fall in the Curriculum, Instruction, and Program Data category.

✴ (30-60 minutes) Using the overhead (created before the activity) of the partially completed Monitoring Checklist from Handout 5.1-2, outline the task for participants: Explain that for each implementation step in the action plan, the team will determine what evidence they will need in order to demonstrate full implementation, who will collect the evidence, and when they will collect it. Have copies of the action plan available for all team members, as well as copies of partially completed Handout 5.1-2 (Monitoring Checklist). Using the overhead to record decisions, work together on a few of the implementation steps in the action plan (listed in the left-hand column).

Then have participants work through the rest of the implementation steps in the plan on their own. Depending on the size of the team, the full team can work together on the remainder of the steps or small groups can each take one or two steps and report out after completing their work. Have participants record their decisions on the same Monitoring Checklist handout. The length of time for the activity will depend on the length of the action plan.

✴ (30 minutes) When participants have finished working on their implementation steps, have them share their decisions. If the whole group has been working on all the steps together, their results will already be documented. If small groups are reporting out, document their decisions on the overhead of the Monitoring Checklist. When the checklist is complete, pass out Handout 5.1-3 (Communicating the Findings). Explain that accountability is ensured and fidelity of implementation is enhanced when results are reported to all stakeholders. Using corresponding Overhead 5.1-4, model filling out the row for one of the stakeholder groups. Depending on the size of the team, the full team can work together to fill out the remainder of the chart, or small groups can each take a stakeholder group and report out after conferring for a short time.

> **Note:** The communication plan completed here is for the monitoring checklist that the group developed to help them answer the question, "Are we doing what we said we would do in our action plan?" If the teams complete Activities 5.2 and 5.3, the communication plan could — and in fact should — be expanded to report findings for the other two questions related to fidelity of implementation and impact on student achievement.

✴ (10 minutes) **Closure:** Quickly review with the teams what was accomplished and what the next steps will be. Brainstorm ways to share the Monitoring Checklist and the Communicating the Findings plan with the full staff.

SELECTING AND DEFINING HIGH-LEVERAGE PRACTICES

Purpose and Objectives

In this activity, a school identifies a few high-leverage practices on which it will focus the most effort for both implementation and monitoring. Doing so helps school staff acknowledge that not all change strategies carry equal value and that those with the greatest direct influence on student achievement are most critical. Defining what successful implementation of each high-leverage practice would look like makes the plan more concrete and provides a basis for developing monitoring tools, such as observation protocols and checklists. In this activity participants

* identify one high-leverage practice for each focus area in the plan, and

* define success criteria for each of these high-leverage practices.

Background for Facilitators

Rationale

In the previous activity, the leadership team outlined a process for answering the question, "Did we do what we said we would do in our action plan?" That process yields information about compliance or completion and, therefore, can be used to hold a school generally accountable for implementing its action plan. It does *not* address the question, "Are we doing the activities in the action plan *well*?" Yet answering this quality-related question for every aspect of an action plan would overwhelm a school and dilute its focus on the most critical areas of the plan.

This activity helps ensure that the school improvement process will maintain a tight focus on a few key areas of critical importance. It reinforces the notion that "doing it all" isn't as important as doing very well the two or three things that will have the greatest influence on student achievement. This activity helps staff members sort through their plan to identify those elements that, if done well, are likely to generate the biggest pay-off in terms of student achievement. Participants learn about the kind of practices that are most likely to provide those payoffs and review their plan to see where they are included. Be aware that an effective practice selected during Activity 4.6 and included in the plan may require several implementation steps.

Defining high-leverage practices will also help teachers and administrators begin to more thoroughly consider what successful implementation will really involve. In addition, because staff themselves define the criteria for success, the monitoring required to track these criteria is less likely to be experienced as an external intrusion and more likely to be understood as an acceptable way of holding themselves accountable to their own vision.

Source

This activity was developed by WestEd facilitators.

139

References

Cohen, D. K., & Ball, D. L. (1999). *Instruction, capacity, and improvement* (Consortium for Policy Research in Education Research Report Series, #RR-043). Philadelphia: Consortium for Policy Research in Education. Available at http://www.cpre.org/Publications/rr43.pdf. Last accessed on June 9, 2006.

Glickman, C. (1993). *Renewing America's schools: A guide for school-based action.* San Francisco: Jossey-Bass Publishers.

National Study of School Evaluation. (2004, September). *Technical guide to school and district factors impacting student learning.* Schaumberg, IL: Author. Available at: http://www.nsse.org/resources_tools/Tech_Guide.pdf. Last accessed June 21, 2006.

Wang, M. C., Haertel, G. D., & Wahlberg, H. J. (1993, December/1994, January). What helps students learn? *Educational Leadership, 51*(4), 74–79.

Ybarra, S., & Hollingsworth, J. (2001, September). Increasing classroom productivity: DataWorks Educational Research's DataWorks Productivity Index. *Leadership.* Available at: http://www.findarticles.com/p/articles/mi_m0HUL/is_1_31/ai_78564790. Last accessed on June 22, 2006.

Uses

This activity should be conducted at the beginning of the school year, when the school is ready to begin implementation and needs to develop monitoring and accountability mechanisms.

These tools can be used either with a school leadership or data team or with an entire school staff. Sometimes the leadership team can identify the high-leverage activities for monitoring and then the staff as a whole can participate in developing criteria for successful implementation. One advantage of involving the whole school in this conversation is that it decreases the likelihood that monitoring or evaluation will be perceived as a threat. It also helps develop a unified set of expectations for both teachers and students. Down the road, it can be useful to point out that the criteria for successful implementation were developed from the ground up rather than being imposed and that the criteria are specific to the school's improvement plan.

Activity Directions

Materials

⇨ Overhead 5.2-1: Educational Impact

⇨ Handout 5.2-1: Selecting the High-Leverage Practices

⇨ Overhead 5.2-2: Selecting the High-Leverage Practices

⇨ Overhead 5.2-3: Defining Success: Examples for Steps 1 and 2 (2 pages)

⇨ Handout 5.2-2: Task Description: Defining Success (2 pages)

⇨ Template 5.2-1: High-Leverage Practice Monitoring Plan

⇨ Template 5.2-2: Defining Success (2 pages)

⇨ Copies of the plan, possibly separated by focus area (see Before the Activity)

⇨ Chart paper and markers

140

Time Required

Approximately 1.5 hours total: 45 minutes to review Overhead 5.2-1 (Educational Impact) and select high-leverage practices, and an additional 45 minutes to develop and record standards for implementation of these practices

Directions for Facilitators

* **Before the Activity:**

    — Determine if Parts 1 and 2 will be done in separate sessions or as a single session. If they will be done separately, determine whether the same participants or different participants will be involved in each part.

    — Determine whether to involve the full staff or just the leadership and/or data team. The activity is likely to be less time-consuming when carried out with a smaller group. On the other hand, working with the entire school staff has the advantage of making this work transparent to everyone from the outset and, also, increasing staff commitment to both implementation and monitoring of the plan.

    — If there are more than 6–8 participants in either part of the activity, divide them into small groups based on the number of high-leverage practices being discussed.

    — Make sufficient copies of the improvement or action plan for all participants or, if you intend to have small groups work on individual focus areas within the plan, make enough copies of each focus area section for participants in the related small group.

    — If you decide to use Option 1 in Part 2 (in which the whole group works on defining success and identifying evidence of success), make a poster of each page of the blank Defining Success form (using Template 5.2-2) for each high-leverage practice or, if you prefer, make an overhead for each one instead. The poster or the overhead will be used for recording ideas generated by the group.

    — If Part 2 will be done as a separate activity, use Template 5.2-2 to make a Defining Success form as a handout for each high-leverage practice identified in Step 1. Fill in the name of the practice, and make enough copies of each one for all participants. Make an overhead of each one as well.

    — Use Template 5.2-1 (High-Leverage Practice Monitoring Plan) to make a monitoring plan form for each high-leverage practice to be discussed in Part 2. If Part 2 is done as a separate activity, fill in the name of the practice (along with timeline and person responsible) on each form, and make enough handouts of each one for all participants.

Part 1: Identifying High-Leverage Practices (45 minutes)

* (10 minutes) Use Overhead 5.2-1 (Educational Impact) to start a discussion about what kinds of educational changes have the largest influence on student achievement. Mention that some changes may be more important in one context than another but that, overall, research shows, changes focused on the classroom have the greatest impact on student achievement. Remind participants of the Cohen and Ball (1999) research showing that the practices having the greatest impact were the ones that not only focused on the classroom but also touched on all aspects of the instructional unit: teacher, student, and materials. Pass out Handout 5.2-1 (Selecting the High-Leverage Practices). Using corresponding Overhead 5.2-2, explain that the process

delineated in the handout is intended to help the team sort through the existing action plan and pick out the high-leverage practices. Explain the importance of focusing on a few practices rather than trying to do everything in the plan very well.

✱ (30 minutes) If all participants are working as a group, give everyone a copy of the whole action plan; if participants are working in small groups, give each small group a copy of a different focus area from the plan (or several focus areas, depending on how many groups you have). Review with participants the directions on Handout 5.2-1 (Selecting the High-Leverage Practices). Have the group(s) discuss and sort the practices in their portion of the plan into the minimal-, medium-, and high-impact categories, recording their rationale or any other notes on the back of the handout. Remind participants of the effective practices that they chose during the plan development phase. Tell them that these practices are now included in the plan but may show up across several implementation steps. Ask the group(s) to select one practice from each focus area (or, in the case of multiple groups, from their own focus area) that they think will have the greatest impact on student achievement and, therefore, should be implemented most carefully and monitored most closely. If necessary, remind participants that to be feasible, the entire monitoring plan can include no more than three high-leverage practices. Again, remind them that a practice, such as providing time for regular teacher collaboration, might be spread across several implementation steps. Tell participants that if time permits, they should begin to consider and describe what successful implementation of their high-leverage practice would look like, taking notes on the back of their handout.

✱ (5 minutes) Ask the group(s) to report on the high-leverage practice(s) they identified and explain why they chose the practice(s). If Part 2 will be done as a separate activity, tell participants what the next steps will be and when Part 2 will take place.

Part 2: Defining Successful Implementation (45 minutes)

✱ (10 minutes) Start by reviewing the three high-leverage practices chosen in Part 1. If different participants are involved at this point, explain how the practices were chosen. Explain that the task now is to "get real" about what success will look like if these activities are effectively implemented and to determine how people will know if this is the case.

✱ (5 minutes) Display and review with participants Overhead 5.2-3 (Defining Success: Examples for Steps 1 and 2). Explain how each descriptor helps the school community clarify what the high-leverage practice will look like when it is implemented with fidelity. Distribute copies of Handout 5.2-2 (Task Description: Defining Success) to help people understand what they will be doing. Explain that in Step 1 they will create descriptors for successful implementation and that in Step 2 they will list the evidence needed in order to know if successful implementation has occurred and will identify how to collect the evidence. Remind participants that their descriptors should include at least one statement about student achievement and direct their attention to an example of this on the overhead. Pass out blank Defining Success forms (from Template 5.2-1). Note: If Parts 1 and 2 are being done in separate sessions, you will have added the names of the practices in advance; if they are being done in the same session, participants will need to write the name of the high-leverage practice in the proper place on the template.

At this point, there are two options, depending on the number of participants. Each one should take approximately 30 minutes.

— **Option 1** (30 minutes) **Whole group defines all high-leverage practices:** For each high-leverage practice, work with the whole group to describe criteria for successful implementation and to identify what evidence should be collected to demonstrate quality implementation. Tell participants that, as a group, they will discuss each high-leverage practice — what success would look like and what evidence would demonstrate success. But tell them that, first, they should each jot down on their Defining Success handouts their own descriptors of success for each practice and what they would consider to be evidence of quality implementation. Tell them to take 5 minutes to note something about all of the high-leverage practices. Tell them to refer to Handout 5.2-2 (Task Description: Defining Success) for more direction on what they should write. After 5 minutes, lead a group discussion of each strategy separately. As the group comes up with ideas, have leadership team members chart descriptors and evidence on the posters prepared before the activity or on an overhead of the blank Defining Success form.

After the charting has been done, show the overhead of the blank High-Leverage Practice Monitoring Plan form (from Template 5.2-1) that participants will complete for one of the high-leverage practices. Explain how, for each high-leverage practice, the success descriptors (from Step 1) and the evidence needed for demonstrating high-quality implementation (from Step 2) will be written on a single form. Tell participants that this completed form will serve as their monitoring plan for the remainder of the year. Determine who will transfer the information from the posters or from the overhead to a High-Leverage Practice Monitoring Plan form for each practice.

— **Option 2** (30 minutes) **Small groups each define one high-leverage practice:** Divide participants into the smaller groups determined before the activity. Have each group select a recorder. Assign one high-leverage practice to each group. Explain that for their respective high-leverage practice, they will be developing descriptors of success and identifying what evidence should be collected to demonstrate high-quality implementation of the practice. If there are more than three groups, two groups may each work on the same practice. Suggest that participants refer to Handout 5.2-2 (Task Description: Defining Success) for more detailed guidance in this work. Give them blank copies of the Defining Success form (from Template 5.2-2) to use for note-taking. Ask the recorder in each group to chart the results of their discussions on the posters created before the activity or on an overhead of the blank form (also created in advance). Give groups approximately 15 minutes to work. Circulate among them to make sure they are filling out the form properly.

If multiple groups are working on the same practice, prior to reconvening the whole group, have them meet to compare notes. Tell them to check to see if they are in agreement or could reach consensus with some additional discussion, and decide what they will report out to the whole group. Tell them to create a single poster or overhead. Have the small groups share their results with the whole group. If more than one small group worked on a single practice, have them share the common chart that they created. Allow time for discussion and commentary.

After the charting is complete, show the overhead of the blank High-Leverage Practice Monitoring Plan (from Template 5.2-1) and explain how, for each high-leverage practice, the descriptors of success (from Step 1) and the evidence needed for demonstrating high-quality implementation (from Step 2) will be written on a single form. Tell participants that this completed form will serve as their monitoring plan for the remainder of the year. Determine who will transfer the information from the posters or from the overhead to a High-Leverage Practice Monitoring Plan form for each practice.

— (5 minutes) **Closure for Options 1 and 2:** Tell participants that all of the implementation steps written into the plan were important. Explain that while, to the best of their ability, they will implement all of those practices and support activities, they have now chosen three high-leverage practices on which to focus most intensely. Tell them that the monitoring plans they created today for the three high-leverage practices will be used throughout the year to evaluate implementation and help ensure that these practices have the intended impact on student achievement.

SETTING INTERIM BENCHMARKS

Purpose and Objectives

Setting benchmarks for student achievement is the final step in creating a complete and coherent monitoring and evaluation process for the school's action plan. In this activity, schools decide what degree of improvement in student achievement they will work toward and expect to see at agreed-upon intervals during the school year. This step commits the school to collecting and analyzing interim assessment data during the school year so midcourse corrections can be made as needed and unpleasant end-of-year surprises can be avoided. Specific objectives for this activity include

* agreement on assessment intervals and expected achievement levels for all students and each subgroup, and

* commitment to regular review of assessment data.

Background for Facilitators

Rationale

This activity lays the foundation for one of the most critical aspects of school reform — looking at results. Research (e.g., Schmoker, 1999) tells us that schools are most likely to improve when they hold themselves accountable for the outcomes of their instructional programs. Completion of the Student Achievement Data template in this activity makes a public statement to staff and other stakeholders about what the school commits to accomplishing and by when. Without this plan for regular examinations of student accomplishment throughout the school year, the action plan can itself become just another document describing things that would be nice to do if anyone had the time.

Certain preconditions must be met before attempting to engage in Activity 5.3. The school must already have agreed-upon assessments to use for capturing interim data about student achievement. Such assessments could be the curriculum-based assessments that often come with a textbook adoption, benchmark assessments developed by teachers or others, or local assessments administered by the district. Whichever ones are used, assessments need to be strongly related to subject-area content and/or performance standards in order to predict student performance on state-administered standards-based assessments.

Subgroup or disaggregated data can and should be represented on the data template. If the purpose of the achievement data is to provide feedback on the effectiveness of program participation (e.g., in a reading intervention or after-school math program), the data must be disaggregated by participation in the given program. Separate targets might be set for different subgroups in order to close achievement gaps. Listing these subgroups ahead of time on the template prompts teams to think about different rates of improvement that must be expected if the gaps are to close.

Decisions about whether to re-administer the same assessment multiple times or to use different but related assessments in a given content area also need to be made ahead of time. Activity 5.3 is focused on the assessment *outcomes*, rather than on the assessments themselves.

145

Source

This activity was developed by WestEd facilitators.

References

Schmoker, M. (1999). *Results: The key to continuous school improvement,* 2nd Ed.). Alexandria, VA: Association for Supervision and Curriculum Development.

Uses

Activity 5.3 can be used either with a school leadership or data team or focus area task forces. It can also be used by the leadership team or focus area task force leaders as a way to lead a conversation with other staff members about expectations.

Activity Directions

Materials

⇨ Overhead 5.3-1: The Importance of Benchmark Data

⇨ Handout 5.3-1: Student Achievement Data Examples (3 pages)

⇨ Overhead 5.3-2: Calendar for Data Review

⇨ Handout 5.3-2: Calendar for Data Review

⇨ Template 5.3-1: Student Achievement Data

⇨ Have the following available as handouts: Copies of the school's student achievement goals; results of baseline assessments, if available; results of most recent standardized assessments; and the assessment calendar for the school and district

Time Required

Approximately 1.5 hours

Plan an optional 30-minute session to follow this activity at which the data template and the monitoring and evaluation process will be presented to the full staff.

Directions for Facilitators

✱ **Before the Activity:** Use Template 5.3-1 (Student Achievement Data) to create a separate data form for each annual achievement goal; fill in any available information, such as school, focus area, annual goal, and which assessment will be used to measure progress. Also fill in any known, related baseline data or subgroup data. If the data are generally disaggregated for specific subgroups but the actual data are not currently available, list the subgroups in the appropriate place on the form. Create an overhead of one of the partially completed forms. Create handouts of all of them.

✱ (15 minutes) Using the overheads of the partially completed Student Achievement Data forms for the annual goals, start by reviewing the student achievement goals already set by the school. Remind participants that these are "end of the road" goals and that the task now is to identify checkpoints for the journey. Make it clear (if necessary) that their role today is not to revisit the goals themselves, which have already been set, but instead to explore how to tell if their improvement efforts are moving in the right direction. Use Overhead 5.3-1 (The Importance of Benchmark Data) to emphasize the value of monitoring student progress in an ongoing manner. Explain that benchmarks should not be randomly set, but should be carefully determined as indicators of progress toward an end-of-year goal. By setting them, the staff is committing to a change process that produces incremental growth as measured by chosen assessments. Using an overhead of one of the partially completed Student Achievement Data forms, explain the task. Give participants Handout 5.3-1 (Student Achievement Data Examples), as well as handouts of each partially completed Student Achievement Data form prepared in advance for the annual achievement goals. Explain how each part of the data template relates to the notion of benchmarks that indicate progress toward the final goal.

✱ (10 minutes) Briefly review the available assessments and recent results. This should include, for example, a quick review of state assessment findings that led to particular student achievement goals, as well as any past local assessment data, including baseline data, if they are available. Using the overhead of a partially completed data form, show where you have recorded these findings.

✱ (10 minutes for explanation and approximately 15 minutes for participants to discuss *each* focus or subject area) Refer participants to the handout of the partially completed data form for whichever annual goal(s) they will be addressing. Explain that for each focus area, they will discuss four things in the following order.

    1) They will briefly discuss the assessment(s) that will be used for benchmarking purposes. In doing so, they should talk, for example, about whether assessment will be cumulative or will test different sets of standards at each administration and whether different versions of one assessment will be given or the same assessment will be given multiple times. Show participants where this information is on their form.

    2) They will discuss how, if at all, data will be disaggregated or for which subgroups data will be collected. Point out where this information is on their form.

    3) They will discuss the baseline level if it has been set. Tell them they should review the baseline levels for the different subgroups. Show participants on the examples where the baseline data are presented for Hidden Valley High and Alta Vista Elementary. If baseline data have not yet been collected, they should either skip this step or note when the baseline assessment will be administered, as in the Earl Warren High School Example.

    4) They will decide what the benchmarks will be for the remaining assessment periods in order to meet their target. If data are disaggregated and a gap exists between some subgroups, they need to be sure that the benchmarks are set in such a way that they will reveal if the gap is closing. In other words, lower-performing subgroups will need to be making more progress than the high-performing subgroups in the same period of time. If the baseline data haven't been collected, participants should set targets based on how much growth they would expect at each benchmark (e.g., at each benchmark there should be a 5 point increase in the percentage of students scoring at the proficient level). Participants can refer to the samples to see examples of this.

✱ (20 minutes) Using Overhead 5.3-2 and Handout 5.3-2 (Calendar for Data Review), have participants determine who will review the data, when, how, and to whom the results will be reported.

* (10 minutes) Have participants plan a presentation to the full staff. Propose the possibility of using the Overhead 5.3-1 (The Importance of Benchmark Data) and having team members share out different parts of the template and the reporting. Be sure to discuss in advance whether changes or additions will be allowed and how the team will handle such requests if they come up.

* (5 minutes) **Closure:** Thank participants for their attention and hard work. Tell them that setting the interim benchmarks is critical to the success of their change efforts. Remind them that over the coming months it will be equally important to adhere to their assessment and monitoring schedule, reviewing the data as soon as it is compiled in case there is a need for midterm adjustments to the plan.

148